100 TIPS
for
Acoustic Guitar

you should have been told

Printed in the United Kingdom by MPG Books, Bodmin

Published by Sanctuary Publishing Limited, Sanctuary House, 45-53 Sinclair
Road, London W14 0NS, United Kingdom

www.sanctuarypublishing.com

Copyright: David Mead, 2002

Photography: Carol Farnworth

Mark Knopfler picture: James Cumpsty

Acoustic guitars by Yamaha

Nylon-string guitars by Admira

ISBN: 1-86074-400-1

100 TIPS
for
Acoustic
Guitar
you should have been told

DAVID MEAD

Other titles available by David Mead from Sanctuary Publishing

Rhythm – A Step By Step Guide To Understanding Rhythm For Guitar
Ten Minute Guitar Workout
100 Guitar Tips You Should Have Been Told
Basic Chords
Basic Scales
Basic Guitar Workout

With Martin Taylor
Kiss And Tell – Autobiography Of A Travelling Musician

ACKNOWLEDGEMENTS

Thanks to Carol Farnworth; my two sons, Timothy and Toby; Martin Taylor for his encouragement and the "Ike" guitar; Darren Power at Yamaha Kemble in the UK; Eric Roche; Jeff Hudson, Chris, Michelle and Penny at Sanctuary Publishing; Tom, Phil, Jeremy, Emmanuelle, Jon and Co at the IGF; and students past and present.

Special thanks to Phil Hilborne for another great-sounding CD, late-night curries and a completely stress-free recording experience.

Finally, I'd like to thank all my friends and family for putting up with scatty, grumpy and precious ol' me while I'm writing and for the understanding, tolerance and love I receive in return.

BOOK CONTENTS

CD CONTENTS

All highlighted items refer to chapter headings. All non-highlighted items refer to examples that can be found as illustrations within a given chapter

David Mead used a Yamaha APXa steel-string acoustic guitar and an Admira nylon-string guitar. Strings were Elixir .12 steel strings and D'addario nylon strings. Microphones were Beyer and Rode. Effects were from Lexicon, Yamaha, Roland and Rocktron. Keyboards/strings played by Phil Hilborne.

Phil Hilborne uses and endorses PRS guitars, Picato strings and Cornford amplification.

FOREWORD

David and I have worked together over many years, first writing a very popular monthly article on jazz guitar in *Guitar Techniques* magazine and later collaborating on my autobiography and guitar-method books. These were all projects that would have been impossible for me to undertake without David's encyclopaedic knowledge of the guitar, his musical understanding, his commitment and his enthusiasm.

David's talents as a guitarist, music educator and author make this book essential reading for the serious guitar student. As with all his publications, this book is written in a clear, no nonsense manner that is designed to demystify many questions that the student may have in a simple, non-challenging way.

Martin Taylor
2002

Martin Taylor and David Mead (RIGHT) performing in Leeds, autumn 2000

INTRODUCTION

"I sometimes go out with a band called Thieves Of Sleep doing stuff stemming from Django, African and Madagascan guitar. We set up hip-hop grooves and I play ethnically confused slide guitar over the top." Bob Brozman

Imagine you're a mechanic standing before the open hood of a car. What you see is a full set of component parts working together to form a single unit – the throbbing heart of that particular automobile: the engine. Now imagine that you have to teach an apprentice how that engine works. You'd do it part by part – this is the carburettor, this is the alternator, and so on. You can probably imagine that, from a novice's point of view, it's very difficult to appreciate how the whole thing works from the aspect of a single part. How does this single bolt fit in the overall concept of "engine"? But if his teacher is any good, the student will trust that one day the whole thing will make some sort of sense and he too will be able to put all the parts together in his mind to form a working whole. He might even be able to suggest a few design modifications along the way and make some sort of a name for himself.

It's the same with music. Basically, I could tell you that music consists of lots of little bits and pieces and that, if you learn to appreciate all of them, you'll end up with a fair appreciation of how it all works, but I realise that sometimes it's difficult to see how some of music's smaller component parts are going to be useful to you, and so I'm going to make you a promise: I won't teach you anything you don't need to know in order to play your acoustic guitar the way you want. So, when I appear to be paying undue attention to a spring-loaded grommet that doesn't actually appear to do anything, you've got to trust me that without this particular component your gleaming, turbo-charged understanding of music isn't going to work. Deal?

Along the way, you're going to meet quite a few physical obstacles, too. Any book on anatomy will show you that playing the guitar asks you to do things with parts of your body that weren't on the original blueprint. Many students of the guitar tend to become discouraged at some of these: the beginner succumbs to blisters on his fretting fingers, barre chords seem almost impossible – the guitar-learning process is full of these and similar bogeymen that will get the better of you unless you manage somehow to keep a sense of humour and laugh in their faces. I'm going to introduce you to many of these guitar-learning demons along the way and I'm going to arm you against them. Our principal weapon here is foreknowledge – knowing your opponent makes him easier to beat, and so I'll take just a minute or so to guide you around the guitar student's armoury.

The "Can't Do" Barrier

This is one of the minor sprites of the guitar kingdom and its main tool of destruction is illogic. You run up against something that you find really, really difficult and you tell yourself, "I can't do this," despite the fact that every other guitar-playing humanoid you come across obviously can, despite the fact that there was probably a time when they, too, were struggling. In all my experience as a teacher, I've found very few actual physical reasons why pupils can't meet most of the demands that the instrument puts upon them. Practically 100 per cent of the time, it's all been down to the self-erected "can't do" barrier. Your best friends in tackling this are your own self-confidence and ingenuity. Learn to recognise the "can't do" beast and avoid its lair at all costs. When encountering something that seems impossible in the early stages, just address the problem in small, well-defined steps and all will be well. Talking to other guitarists will often reveal that they've experienced exactly the same hang-up or problem as you over some area of technique or musical understanding. They overcame it and didn't look back. So can you.

The "Personal Everest" Syndrome

Want to go mountain climbing? Fine. Common sense tells you not to take on anything that's beyond your experience or you're probably not going to have too good a time of things. Worse still, you could end up in serious trouble and become fatally involved with Newton's Law of Gravity. So why do so many guitar students set themselves impossible tasks and lose all sense of morale when they inevitably fail? I've seen it so often that I gave it a name: the Personal Everest syndrome. Your talisman here is a sense of proportion – take small, measured paces and don't set yourself unreasonable agendas. A good teacher will recognise a pupil who is reaching beyond his abilities and will try to keep things on an even keel while offering tempered words of encouragement at the same time. So there will be times when the snow goggles and high-altitude breathing apparatus have to remain in the cupboard in the interests of actually making real progress in the foothills.

The Three Ps (A Pep Talk)

These stand for Patience, Persistence and Practice, the three attributes that will ward off even the most awkward S-bends that music can throw in your path. I've seen quite a few students falter because they became impatient with their own fumbling development on the instrument, despite reassurances from me that we've all been there at one time or another and managed to dig ourselves out, mainly via help from the Three Ps.

In the early stages of learning any new technique, there is going to be a period when it's just a chore – simply that. Nobody likes practising things they can't make any sense out of, and so these things tend to be put on the back burner in the practice room and not given the attention they need. As a teacher, I have to gently remind students that I promised not to teach them anything they're not going to need and that practising this or that is going to benefit them in areas which perhaps they've been unable to appreciate.

Most of us would agree that it's possible to enjoy driving but that the enjoyment factor only really kicks in after you've gone through the laborious task of actually learning to drive. Can you remember when driving was just a series of separate actions that you had to learn to co-ordinate? Can you remember thinking that it was always going to feel foreign and strange and perhaps slightly scary at the same time? And yet now driving is instinctive – you don't have to think about it; you just get in the car and drive. Needless to say, playing guitar is very similar. In the early stages, there are all sorts of unfamiliar disciplines and muscle-challenging routines that you have to become used to and it's difficult to foresee a day when playing itself becomes relatively carefree and enjoyable, but it does happen, just the same as it did when you learned to drive. The things you called upon then – which would have involved healthy doses of the Three Ps – are there to be called upon now. Don't give up!

The Quirk Factor

This is another syndrome that I make sure I point out to everyone I teach. The quirk factor is one of those annoying facts of guitar life that dogs a teacher continuously. Let's put it this way: if you asked me to teach you something on the guitar – a technique, a chord arrangement or a complete piece – naturally I'm going to teach you the way that I think is the most approachable. I'm not going to teach you to scale cliffs wearing roller blades, let's put it that way. However, the guy who wrote the piece or played the guitar part in the first place is going to play it the way he learned it, irrespective of the fact that he might be contravening most of music's minor laws (and a couple of major ones) along the way. In other words, his way might not be the most straightforward available. As an example, I would never show someone how to play a Dire Straits guitar part using Knopfler's original right-hand fingering. Mark plants two fingers down on the body of the guitar and picks with his remaining fingers and thumb. Fine – it works for him, but have you tried it? Instant hand cramp and very bad playing habits start here. This is where the quirk factor comes into play – Knopfler's right-hand fingering quirk works for him, but it won't work for you.

This is only one example, of course, and you'll find hundreds more along the way. What I ask is that you always ask yourself the question, "Is there a better or easier method?" In this way, you're going to be accommodating quirks of your own and striking out on the path towards becoming an individual musician.

Another Promise

One last thing. If you're anything like me (and in some ways I truly hope you're not), you hate reading books that are encrusted with jargon and buzz-words that you need some kind of insider info or a dedicated dictionary to work out. Music is absolutely chock full of it and, just to make successive generations of guitar students mad, some of our jargon has been translated into different languages – we've got Latin, French, Italian, German, Greek, you name it – so I generally make a promise in the books I write that I will only ever use jargon if I offer a full explanation as well, because I believe it really is crucial that you're aware of this particular buzz-word's existence. Otherwise, we'll speak English, if that's OK with you.

Tips From The Top

Throughout this book, you'll find quotes from some of the world's best players taken from interviews I spent ten years putting together as a guitar-magazine journalist. Some of them are extremely relevant to the accompanying text while others are one-liners that offer surprising insight into playing in general, but all are here to uplift and inspire you in your studies. I hope you'll find some answers to the acoustic-guitar puzzle within these pages. Good luck!

BEGINNINGS

"My first guitar was a Hoyer, from Bell's in Surbiton. It looked like a gut-stringed guitar, but it was steel stringed. An odd combination." Eric Clapton

As you'll probably have realised by now, one of the things that makes the guitar so confounding is that there doesn't seem to be too much definition between doing things the "right way" and the "wrong way", as far as going about the task of learning how to play it is concerned. Something that works for one player won't for another and, in general, we're left standing there with bemused puzzlement, not really knowing how to make a positive start.

As a further introduction to the subject of learning the instrument, I thought it would be interesting to collect together quotes from many of the voices featured throughout this book on the common theme of what got them started as players. You'll find diversity, much irregularity and, hopefully, inspiration in knowing that there are many paths towards competence as a player.

"I got involved with folk music because I couldn't afford an amplifier and so I couldn't be in a beat group like I desperately wanted to be. Bob Dylan told me that he was in the same boat – he really wanted to be Little Richard, but he couldn't do that." *Mark Knopfler*

"I was learning pieces from the student classical repertoire – Carcassi and Bach, some of the old English composers, all those typical things that every kid classical player goes through. After a while, I started discovering things and tried to incorporate them into my playing. I decided there

were enough classical players out there and so I started to write my own stuff." *Ottmar Liebert*

"My initial early guitar playing stuff came out of folk music – Pete Seeger and all sorts of other people. I was given a record by my parents called *The Pete Seeger Guitar Tutor Record*. Lesson one is how to tune the thing, then it teaches you a few chords, and I never got beyond the third lesson! Thereafter I would sit up and listen to Radio Luxembourg on headphones late at night, trying to work out the bass, rhythm and lead guitar parts of every record that came on.

"The first guitar I got was a Spanish guitar. I borrowed it from a friend and never gave it back. I think." *David Gilmour*

"I think it was Brazilian music which took me to the nylon string. When I was a teenager, I was listening to a lot of Latin and Brazilian music – those lovely chords on the nylon string just had a better sound – but my first guide was my uncle, who was a great guitarist and accordionist. He used to play all these lovely waltzes and tangos – dancing music, but with a great European melody. I think I learned a lot about structure, songs and melody then. It was a very formative time for me." *Antonio Forcione*

"I stumbled on this Johnny Winter album where he was playing resonator guitar and I became fascinated with the sound and by the look of the thing. I went into town and bought one in 1967 and that's the same one I'm playing now. Once I realised where Johnny Winter was getting his source material from, I just went to the source – that was it. So, basically, the first time I listened to Johnny Winter was also the last time. From then on, I went diving into the usual Mississippi suspects." *Bob Brozman*

"Well, I learned a lot of my stuff from the late Guitar Slim and some of the great guitar players and horn players and keyboard players. I saw that actions speak louder than words, and I never thought I was a real good guitar player or a real good singer, so the late Guitar Slim used to show me some stuff – you know, he would go and hit his guitar, and if he stepped off the stage these people were, like, eating it up." *Buddy Guy*

"The first guitar would have been a Spanish or Brazilian guitar. I didn't touch a steel-string for years. I started with all the basic chords – Beatles and things like that – but I've always liked Brazilian music and had an understanding for Latin music, so I've tended to apply it to everything I do." *Dominic Miller*

"I had this horrible guitar that cut my fingers all up. It was a cheap old steel-string guitar that frustrated me no end, but for some reason I stayed with it. Fortunately, not so long afterwards, I had access to the guitars that my dad had around the house. I started playing nylon-string around then and went through a long period of playing that. I must have been really stubborn about wanting to play the guitar because I was not encouraged by the instrument I had. It was painful! But in hindsight it was good and the people who were our heroes also played on primitive and very difficult-to-play instruments and ultimately made glorious music, and so there's something to it." *Eric Bibb*

"The action was terrible – you had to be Arnold Schwarzenegger to hold a chord down! I had

big black grooves in my fingers from trying to hold down simple little chords on the thing. But I had a guitar and I was totally into it, and that marked the beginning of the process, y'know?" *Jim Mullen on his first guitar*

"My dad brought me to hear Big Bill Broonzy when I was nine. He was a friend of Bill's and I just felt completely awed by this giant of a man who was so gentle and his playing was just unbelievable. Then, when I was ten or eleven years old, I got a Sonny Terry And Brownie McGhee album – it was actually a ten-inch LP – and it sowed the seeds, I suppose. When I was in my early teens, I heard Chuck Berry, Ray Charles, Bo Diddley and Little Richard on the radio, and they were all great R&B artists back then and so dynamic. Then, in 1957, I got an album called *The Country Blues* which was produced by Sam Charters and was a compilation album of artists from the '20s and '30s. There was Robert Johnson, Leroy Carr, Blind Boy Fuller, Blind Willie McTell, Blind Lemon… It was an extraordinary album and I'd not heard the old stuff before, and that was my major inspiration to actually want to play myself.

"When you hear a guitar player whose guitar and voice are sort of interweaved to make this incredible painting – I don't know how exactly to word it – it becomes so crucial to the song. I didn't play an instrument until I was 18 and then I started playing professionally when I was 19, so it kind of hit me all at once. But there had been years of this thing festering inside me, and so when I got my first guitar, that was it." *John Hammond*

"My stepfather, he just taught me his style, a sort of rhythm-and-lead style. It's a strange style." *John Lee Hooker*

"I can't really remember the earliest time that my father put a guitar in my hands, except that I've seen photographs of it. I can't remember anything from the age of four; my earliest memories are from around the age of eight. I can remember practising and the house we were living in then. I had a daily half-hour routine and my father told me not to wiggle my thumb and to keep my fingers in position. I remember, too, a tape I made around the age of eight which I sent to my grandparents in England – just a few little pieces, but it was actually quite good! So I was obviously playing fairly well by then, and it's a kind of irony that I can't remember what led up to it." *John Williams*

"A friend of mine who lived across the road got a guitar, and when I saw that I thought that was really what I wanted, and so my dad bought me a guitar. It was made in Russia and was like a classical guitar only it had steel strings on with an absolutely horrific action! But I got this guitar and I just couldn't put it down. I just became obsessed with it and I just played all weekend and I couldn't wait to get back from school to start playing again." *Martin Taylor*

"I started off basically because I had noticed that guys who had guitars were accompanied by girls who were a hell of a lot better looking than the ones I was getting, if I was getting any at all. From the guitar players I've talked to, that seems to be a universal reason for wanting one. People as diverse as Mick Ronson and John Fahey have said the same thing.

"I pestered my mother to get me a six-quid guitar. It was a reddish colour and just about impossible to play, from what I remember. Then we started this skiffle group.

"There was one guy in Kitchen's shop in Leeds who taught classical guitar with a bit of flamenco, if you weren't careful, and that was it. As long as I could play E and A and B – and then, when I got to G and C and D – I thought I was king of the world! Then someone said, 'You can mix them up a bit, if you like. I think that's what this guy's doing.' And he played me a John Lee Hooker record. He was only playing E and G, if you were lucky, and sometimes it was just E, and so I thought, 'Well, that's all

right.' I'd been watching people on television and the big revelation was after I'd been watching Tommy Steele and a French guy called Henri Salvador. They just had a guitar strung around their necks and people in the backline playing for them. I didn't know about things like that back then; I thought that you just strung it around your neck and off it went. I tried that for about ten days until a guy who lived a couple of miles away who had a guitar told me that I had to use the other hand as well! I said, 'Don't be daft. That's going to make it impossible.' But the horrible thing was that he turned out to be right. But once I'd got through the simple, basic chords, I found that it was amazing what you can play." *Michael Chapman*

"So much of the music that I loved was guitar-based. After I'd been playing keyboards for a few years, I realised that I couldn't produce all the tones that I wanted to hear on that instrument, so I figured that I needed to head off in another direction. So I asked my parents for a guitar for my eleventh birthday. I was literally just trying to make things up and just trying to get a familiarity with the fretboard and picking out melodies to songs that I liked. I must have got a list of chord shapes at some point because I started to figure out the chords – just simple formations. But I remember doing a lot of writing straight away when I got the guitar. I found it easy to move my fingers up and down and invent melodies and so forth." *Mike Keneally*

"I picked it up somewhere around seven or eight years old. It's hard to pinpoint exactly. I come from a very musical family – my father was an opera singer, my mother was a classically trained pianist and my brother was a trumpet player, and so for me I think it was just a case of wanting to join in!

"I was a folkie. I listened to Pentangle, The Incredible String Band, Tom Paxton and Eric Anderson. I was also into country-blues people like Mississippi John Hurt and the Reverend Gary

Davis and I was keen on the ragtime style of guitar playing, going after the Scott Joplin rags and stuff… I didn't pick up an electric guitar until I was about 14 or 15 years old, and I started playing with other people around the same time. That's when I got my first real whiff of rock 'n' roll and it was all over for me." *Nick Kane, The Mavericks*

"My father talked me into it. I actually wanted to be an illustrator – I wanted to draw – so I would come home from school every day and do my homework, then listen to music and just draw. My father thought I was too serious about my school work and wanted to find something that would make me more social. He had a friend who played guitar with Tommy Dorsey and Paul Anka and he gave lessons, and so I started playing. I don't think there would be too many kids whose parents worry that they're too much into their school work!" *Reeves Gabrels, The David Bowie Band*

"I have two older sisters and they were big Beatles and Rolling Stones fans, and I just got into playing guitar that way. Then the first thing that turned me on to the blues really was probably a Lightnin' Hopkins album my sister had. It was the first proper blues I heard; I'd heard Eric Clapton and Jimi Hendrix playing bluesy stuff, but that was the first proper blues I heard.

"I started playing when I was about ten, then I started classical guitar for about four years from the age of about 14 to 18. It was my mum that wanted me to do that. She thought that being taught 'properly' would be the thing, and I enjoyed it for the most part. I'd get a bit hacked off having to practise and learn scales and stuff now and again, though. I did all the grade exams and passed Grade Eight, then I joined a band. I didn't go to music college, so I never got a full formal musical education, but I learned to read a bit and learned to use my right hand, so I was grateful for that." *Robbie McIntosh, The Paul McCartney Band/The Pretenders*

"Everybody in my street had a guitar and all we did was listen to the radio and try to steal everything we could from the radio. Also, my parents had a great record collection when I was growing up, and it wasn't until I started hanging out with some of my friends when I went to high school, at about 15 or 16 years old, that I went back to my parents' record collection. At that age, I had some friends who were listening to Buddy Guy and BB King, and so we started hanging out together and listening to their records and it all went from there." *Robert Cray*

"I started playing at the age of nine, and that was due to one of the tutors – Granville Shaw – at the school I was at, the Mansell Middle School. He was the geography teacher and maths teacher, but he also had an ABRSM qualification in music on the piano. But he was a big fan of the guitar and he actually had a little guitar orchestral group at lunchtimes and at break times, so it kind of attracted me to the guitar, especially playing in a group of other students. I was really attracted to the sound and the versatility of the instrument more than anything else, and he played me a recording of Andrés Segovia and that really impressed me enormously. I had played the recorder and tried the flute before then, but that was the real start for me.

"There was a big music scene in Sheffield then and I had electric-guitar lessons at the same time as I was having classical-guitar lessons, but I found that for me, personally, the classical guitar just had that little bit more to offer. I suppose the history of the instrument stems back to the Renaissance period, and there is such a variety of music available, although I was greatly influenced by the music around me, particularly rock music. Sheffield at that time was a hotbed for major rock bands such as Iron Maiden, Def Leppard, Saxon and all those kinds of rock bands. I was surrounded by it because the other pupils at the school were listening to heavy rock and obviously the new romantics were just coming up in that period as well. In a way, Sheffield dominated that, too, for a short period of time with The Human League, Heaven 17 and ABC, and I followed that as well, but deep down inside classical was the road I was clearly going to take." *Simon Dinnigan, classical guitarist*

"I was actually quite young when my brother and I started to entertain the family with one of those plastic Elvis Presley guitars. After the dog chewed it up, my brother moved onto ukulele, but I always had this thing for guitar from very early on. Scotty Moore was my hero, and this would be around the time that we were living in Mississippi, but then we moved to Louisiana when I was seven years old. My first real guitar was a big Kay acoustic, and I'm sure it was incredibly hard to play." *Sonny Landreth*

"There's a picture that was taken of me when I was about five years old – I'm playing a little five-dollar guitar. That must have been around '51 or '52. I had discovered country music at that age and I was listening to it a lot in my room. Mostly, I was attracted to the bluegrass element of it – all those post-war great artists from when bluegrass was in its heyday. I also started listening to Wolfman Jack out of Texas, and he played all those gutbucket blues by black guys who I'd never heard of.

"I learned by playing and asking other players to show me things, which they would, back then. I wanted to progress on banjo and I took a few lessons from a classical guitarist based in Washington called Sophocles Papas, who had been a student of Segovia's. We had a banjo book which was written by an Englishman, and I still can't figure out what an English guy knows about bluegrass! But the tablature was a bitch to read and Sophocles would try to walk me through all this, but every so often he would hand me a nylon-string guitar and ask me if I'd ever considered learning guitar. I told him I already played and he asked me to play him something, so I played him a really amateurish version of 'Malaguena' and his advice was to screw the banjo and concentrate on playing guitar. But I was determined to stick with the banjo; I preferred the more popular art forms!" *Tim Rose*

"I started playing in 1959, when I was four years old. My mother showed me my first few chords – she played a little bit of lap-steel guitar and sang a little and so she got me started by buying me a cheap guitar and showing me a few things on it, and that kept me inspired for a long time. My father was helping out local bands in the area; some of them would come over and rehearse in our living room at weekends, so my brother, Phil, and I were down on our hands and knees in front of the guys' amplifiers listening to music by bands like The Shadows, The Ventures, Duane Eddy and things like that.

"Then, when I was seven years old, I heard Chet [Atkins] playing a solo piece called 'Windy And Warm', and that was a real turning point for me because, even at that early age, I realised that he was playing everything at once and that it was a self-contained style, so I set about trying to work it out when I was a kid. I started playing fingerstyle using a pick as well, because I didn't realise that Chet was using a thumbpick, and so I worked out a few tunes when I was a kid, like 'Freight Train' and 'Trambone', but using a plectrum. Then, in '65, I was given the *Best Of Chet Atkins* album by a friend of the family, and of course there he is on the cover with a thumbpick. So I took a look at it and thought, 'That's it!' That helped me to get better at playing that style, by utilising the thumb properly." *Tommy Emmanuel*

"I guess the thing that drew my ear to the guitar in the first place was the folk boom in America in the early '60s. I was listening to Peter, Paul And Mary and The Chad Mitchell Trio – I was a big fan of theirs. Then Bob Dylan's first album really caught my ear. So I wanted to get a guitar and go to parties, strum and sing 'Michael, Row The Boat Ashore' – all those songs you learn as a kid and sit around a campfire and sing." *Walter Trout*

"When I was about eight years old, I was very influenced by soul music – Otis Redding, James Brown, The Four Tops and The Temptations. Then, when I heard Cream and Jimi Hendrix and that kinda stuff, that's what made me want to start playing guitar." *Warren Haynes, The Allman Brothers Band and Gov't Mule*

"[My first guitar] was a three-quarter-sized nylon-string classical guitar. At school, they had a guitar club, and I think my dad went into the school and asked them what they thought he should buy me and they recommended a make which was cheap and good. So I went to the club and various get-togethers at school, but what they were playing was fairly simple – easy chords and stuff. Basically, I wanted to play the sort of stuff I heard on my dad's records, and so I worked it out on my own.

"I listened to a lot of Clapton when I was younger, and he was probably the first guitarist I tried to be like. I learned all the solos from *Bluesbreakers* and pieces like 'Hideaway' note for note and tried to play them on this classical guitar, bending the strings and stuff! When I was ten, my parents bought me my first electric guitar, which was a Strat copy, and that allowed me to go onto the next level of playing solos. So, for the first few years, Clapton was everything." *Aynsley Lister*

"Lonnie Donegan was my hero in those days, and so I tried to work out his songs on a ukulele,

and it didn't work. I managed later that year to get my mother to buy me a round-hole steel-string guitar." *Al Stewart*

"My father used to play folk and blues and stuff and guitarists were always coming round to the house and jamming, so I gradually took the guitar up and started doing gigs with him. Actually, I did my first gig when I was nine! One day, I heard Django Reinhardt and I was just knocked out by his approach to the guitar." *Neil Stacey*

"I liked it because it was so tinny-sounding. It was just an acoustic guitar, but it was moving closer to that wiry tone I liked with Johnny 'Guitar' Watson, especially if you picked it right next to the bridge." *Frank Zappa on his first guitar*

"If I can add my own voice to this collection, I wanted a guitar – quite desperately – from when I was about nine or ten, but it took me ages to convince my parents that this would be a worthwhile investment. Alas, the capriciousness of youth had seen me through many fads and fancies and I suspect our loft was probably still full of most of them.

"In the end, I had piano lessons, which I hated, and it was my teacher's frustration that finally led me to finding a guitar-shaped package under the Christmas tree one year. It was condemned by my mother as being another of my 'seven-day wonders', of course. But that was 30 years ago…" *David Mead*

THE ACOUSTIC RENAISSANCE

"I must admit, I found it all a little bit overblown. I mean, I thought the album was quite rough, to say the least." *Eric Clapton talking about his multiple Grammy Awards for his* Unplugged *album*

From my position as music journalist and guitar-magazine editor, I suppose I was lucky enough to have something of a grandstand view of the twists and turns taken by the guitar over the past ten years or so. Every morning, the postbag threw up CDs and press releases from aspiring new acts hoping to gain my attention long enough to consider running a feature on them. Time and experience taught me that the more desperate they were, the more the music was hopelessly derivative, trendy and directionless. And some of the measures used by record companies to get journalists to listen to albums were hilarious. I was sent a fresh orange in a box through the post once along with a suitably eager, squeaky-keen press release telling me about this week's "next big thing" in the music world. I ate the orange – as far as I remember, it was very nice – but I don't remember the music it was supposed to help promote.

Apologies for sounding so cynical. It's just what ten years in music journalism does for you.

The point I'm trying to get across here is that sometimes I would hear something that really was refreshing – and it was never accompanied by an orange. It didn't need to be. I heard several CDs that reminded me why I was a musician first and foremost, but the chills and thrills were comparatively rare and time after time it was an acoustic musician who was responsible for the goosebumps.

So, from my position in the crow's nest, I scanned the horizon and gradually became aware of a new acoustic-guitar movement, a new generation who had learned from the likes of the late Michael Hedges that

there were no boundaries to the instrument and leaps forward were there to be taken.

If we backtrack for a few moments, the acoustic guitar probably appeared on the map in the hands of singer/songwriters like Paul Simon, Joni Mitchell, James Taylor, Bob Dylan and others like them. In those days, the guitar itself was secondary to the songs, merely a device that accompanied a tune. You could add a full band, even an orchestra or two, but the artists were still defined as acoustic acts.

Then there came the acoustic virtuosi, guitarists who played complete pieces – instrumental pieces – on their instruments. Early pioneers included Michael Chapman, Ralph McTell, Isaac Guillory and Gordon Giltrap, but they were considered part of a specialist minority market, despite doing well on the club scene. In fact, they were all lumped together into the folk bracket, which was a pigeonhole that they, and others like them, would occupy for a couple of decades.

I don't know exactly when it was that the revolution in acoustic guitar really began. Once again, my position as guitar-magazine editor revealed that sales of electric guitars were falling and those acoustic guitars were on the incline. This may have had something to do with the fact that, in general, acoustic guitars were now better produced. When I started learning, the only budget acoustics on the market were kind to the purse but cruel to the ears and fingers. How many times have you heard guitarists say that they started learning on an acoustic guitar that would have made the Marquis de Sade roll around the floor in delight? With playing actions as high as you like, fretboards you could grate cheese with and all the tone of a wasp in a jam jar, my generation had no choice but to pay up and shut up.

At the dawn of the 1990s, however, things had changed to the point where you could buy a modestly priced instrument and begin to learn to play without too much physical pain involved. Luxury. Sheer luxury.

This fact might have been responsible for the change of pace in the acoustic-music market. I don't know. It would certainly be a factor, however, and it remains one today.

I suppose the other thing that drew public consciousness away from the clamour of electric guitardom was the "Unplugged" series run on MTV. At the time, it was quite a radical idea – take a well-known rock act, confiscate their electric identity and throw them onstage with purely acoustic weaponry.

Some of the shows were memorably good while some we'd probably better not talk about, but the idea was set in motion and, in some respects, the acoustic guitar was reborn.

Now, I believe that, if you want to see and hear fresh innovation on the guitar, you need only seek out an acoustic performer. There are plenty of them around, all quietly pushing the boundaries of what was once considered possible on the instrument to the extent that classical guitar is now far from the only area of guitar playing where polyphonic virtuosity can be taken for granted. It is to these pioneers of acoustic guitar's new age that I humbly dedicate this book. I hope that the musicians they inspire will move forward to make their own music, aware that now there are no rules, no boundaries and that pretty much anything is possible.

READING TABLATURE

"There were musicals like *Jesus Christ Superstar* and I played in the pit for a while in that, having learned all the songs from tape and making out that I was reading them every night." *Tommy Emmanuel*

These days, the question "Should I learn to read music?" is not as familiar among guitarists as it was just a short time ago. For years, learning to understand music notation was thought to be the only proper way of transferring the written page to the fretboard and anything else was thought of as being decidedly dodgy, to say the least. But for a very long time, the only form of guitar music that tended to be written down in the first place was for classical guitar. Everything else was really quite hopeless, in that it represented the time-honoured (and now thankfully out-of-favour) system of writing material that was considered to be "popular music" (and by that I mean everything from James Taylor to AC/DC) for piano with a somewhat haphazard and usually mournfully inept attempt at supplying chord boxes. Various pupils of mine were dismayed to discover that even very famous and bestselling albums like Dire Straits' *Brothers In Arms* were written out for piano only and subsequently of no real use to them. To make matters worse, the chords were usually wrong, too.

In the mid '80s, things began to change. Music-book publishers started to realise that guitarists weren't happy with merely playing the wrong chords to an album track; they wanted the actual notes played by the original guitarist himself. It was in this way that tablature – a dedicated system of writing music for the guitar – enjoyed something of a renaissance. Suddenly, whole albums were available in tablature (or "tab" for short), and at long last renditions of 'Money For Nothing' were pretty much on target.

Of course, I'm not saying that tab was a new thing discovered by the guitar adventurers of the '80s – far from it. Tab first saw the light of day around 400 years ago, when music traditions were very different indeed. (If you ever find yourself in the vicinity of the British Museum, you'll be able to see some tablature from the early 18th century, for instance.) The reason why tab fell into disfavour back then was because it was such an exclusive system. Only guitarists (well, lutenists) could read it, and it was about as far as you could get from the far more universally understandable form of standard notation. So guitarists had to toe the line somewhat and abandon tab altogether. This, of course, meant that they had to grapple with some of the guitar's weirder attributes – for instance, there are five places on the instrument where it's possible to play middle C. Whereas tab would have told you the intended position instantly, readers of standard notation had to work it out for themselves in relation to what had just happened in the music they were playing and, naturally, what came next. All of a sudden, the job got harder.

Centuries later, tab was adopted once more as an incredibly useful tool for the guitar student. I've proved to many students how it's possible to learn to read tab in a single lesson, whereas it can take around six months to become a useful music reader.

"I'm a studied musician. I went to Berklee for about ten minutes!" *David Torn*

Become A Tab Reader

Basically, tab consists of six horizontal lines, representing the strings of the guitar, and it looks like this:

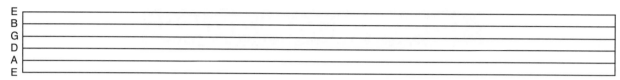

Example 1

The bass E string is at the bottom, which means that the next five lines correspond to the A, D, G, B and E strings respectively. As far as what goes where is concerned, a simple numbering system indicates the fret upon which you're expected to play a note. Study the diagram below:

Track 2

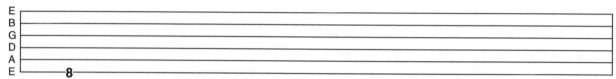

Example 2

This shows the figure "8" on the bass E string. If you were to play the note on the eighth fret of your E string, you'd end up with a C. Try it.

So much for single notes. What about melodies or scales? They'd be shown like this, a series of numbers reading sequentially left to right:

Track 2

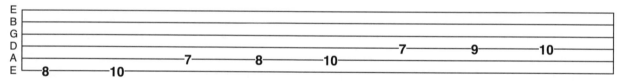

Example 3

The example above is a C-major scale. (Check the CD if the methodology still seems mysterious.) If the music calls for you to play two or more notes simultaneously, the numbers are stacked vertically, like this:

Track 2

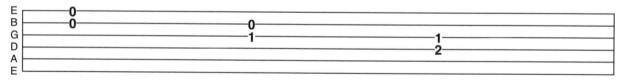

Example 4

Once again, the CD will come to your aid if things don't quite make sense. The example above shows two notes played at once, but if whole chords are represented, they look like this:

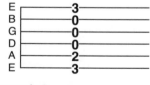

Track 2

Example 5

This totem-pole of numerals might look a little daunting at first, but take it slowly and read from the bottom upwards and you'll soon acquire the knack. The chord above is a G major which will arguably look far more familiar to you if presented in chord box form, thus:

Believe it or not, that's really all there is to it. Of course, it will take a while for you to become fluent with tab, but it's not such a hard system to come to terms with. It's certainly easier than standard notation!

Author's Message

If there are any drawbacks to reading tab it is firstly that it contains no rhythmic information, and so, whereas you can be sure that you're putting your fingers in all the right places, tab still stops just short of telling you the whole story. This means that it's very difficult to look at the tab version of a tune or solo that you aren't familiar with and play it straight away. That said, it really is useful as a guide to a piece that you've got in your record collection and have been yearning to play yourself.

My advice is to treat tab as a quick fix and not so much as a means to an end. It's also no substitute for standard notation if you're going to be in a position where reading music is expected of you – in examinations, for instance, and in some band situations. But rest assured that learning standard notation is only necessary if it's going to be useful to you. It's far from obligatory.

I've used tab exclusively in this book in order to make the examples and pieces as instantly and as universally accessible as possible. After working through the exercises and examples in the other chapters, you should find that your tab-reading capabilities will allow you to venture out there into a whole world of notated music and – with patient, persistent practice, of course – you'll be able to unlock all of its secrets.

A WORD ABOUT PRACTICE

"You just practise that thing as best as you can and listen to all music. You get ideas from everything and you wake up one morning and you have something you've created." Buddy Guy

You've probably read all the stories about practice bravado and all the derring-do associated with long hours spent in front of a metronome with a guitar in hand, and they're probably all true, but back here in the real world a question commonly asked would be something like, "How much practice do I need to do?", which translates to, "What is the absolute minimum I can actually get away with so I can still lead a relatively normal life?" The answer is about ten minutes a day, which surprises a lot of people – or at least it does until I explain how I differentiate between the words *practice* and *noodling*.

If we're honest, most of the time we spend allegedly practising is actually wasted. Simply playing through your favourite licks and a couple of party pieces while perched on the sofa in front of the TV isn't practising; it's known in the guitar-teaching trade as noodling. Practice is far more regimented than that, but that doesn't mean it isn't rewarding or even (gulp!) fun. I used to have a bargain with my students: the first ten minutes of their hour-long lesson were mine, while the other 50 minutes were all theirs. This meant, in effect, that I'd spend the first ten minutes taking them through what they should be practising on a technical level and recommend additions and alterations and provide help with problems, etc. After that, we could do anything they liked – if they wanted a song written out, fine; if they wanted a solo transcribed, equally fine. All I needed to know was that their technical skills were developing nicely first, and then we could work on their own musical development via exploring the material that they wanted to learn.

What this meant was that the students who didn't practise at all, or at best maybe went through a few scales just before they came out for their lesson, wasted a lot of their time because they were invariably slow with the technical exercises. But the carrot-and-stick approach usually worked, as learning songs and solos, etc, usually took precedence, and so they'd complete their part of the bargain as a means to an end. I didn't think – and still don't – that ten minutes is too much time to spend in some sort of daily practice routine, as long as it's serving you in developing all of the necessary skills you'll need to play what you want.

In fact, while we're on the subject, I'll shamelessly plug my own book *Guitar Workout* (that's *Ten Minute Guitar Workout* in the US), which streamlines practice by condensing it into a progressive ten-minute-a-day plan. After that, noodle away, but with any luck you'll be thirsty for further challenges.

"It's often people with a background in martial arts who understand what we're doing rather than someone who is perhaps a professional guitar teacher, because someone in the martial arts very quickly learns about having a centre of gravity. A guitarist sits on a chair for four hours and he must have a centre of gravity, too. In martial arts, if you are slightly off in either direction, then you will have a bloody nose. In aikido, you will be on the mat, so someone with a martial-arts background understands when I put a lot of time and attention into holding the pick. They know why – it's not arbitrary, it's not anal retention, it's not being finicky; it's that, if in the left hand there is no centre of gravity, if in the right hand there is no centre of gravity, if in the body there is no centre of gravity, you will not be playing that exercise for more than ten minutes because the tension will be excruciating. If the right hand is out of balance, then you'll hear a horrible, nasty scraping sound as the pick scrapes across the wound strings. In martial arts, you'll be on the floor or have a bleeding nose." *Robert Fripp*

Practice should be challenging. It should never be reduced to static repetition and should constantly evolve and progress so that you always have something fresh to learn. Too many people want to get practice out of the way so that they can get down to some "real playing", and so they see it as an obstacle, a chore that has to be done.

I used to ask some students if polishing their cars was a chore. Most of them agreed that it was, but they were rewarded in the end by the positive result of seeing nice shiny cars. I told them to imagine that they were doing the same to their guitar playing. In the end, they'd have nice shiny techniques. It worked with some, but the ones who wanted instant gratification were often not so easy to convince.

Your Practice Environment

A lot of people don't necessarily give too much thought about where they should practise. Like I say, in front of the TV seems to be the consensus, but that's definitely not an environment fit for learning. (It still amazes me how one of the greatest mass-communication tools ever invented should be turned over to entertainment. Sadly, the Internet seems to be going the same way.)

Ideally, you should be alone when you practise – and no, I haven't been speaking to the other members of your family; I mean in general. This requirement is often overlooked out of necessity because of the general layout of most homes, but isolation is the best possible thing, if at all possible. This means that there are no distractions – critical spouses who have heard

you play the beginning of 'Stairway To Heaven' once too often, younger or older brothers and sisters who lay in wait to snipe at every goof you make, parents who rue the day you ever saw that guitar in the local music-shop window and so on. We've all been there, trust me.

So, if possible, find a quiet place with no distractions, sit in a sensible chair (sofas are an absolute no-no) and get down to the job in hand.

Posture

"With classical hand positions, it's impossible to stand up and play a Bach fugue; it is impossible to get the right rhythmic feel into the arm and right hand for fast single-note improvising." *John Williams*

The most important thing you can do when you start any kind of serious practising is to take a good look at your posture. We'll see later how important it is to rid the arms, hands and so on of any undue tension, and the same has to be said for the rest of your body. The guitar makes certain demands on the body that biology tries to defend at every turn. For instance, the guitar encourages you to stoop over the instrument while sitting down (look at yourself in a mirror if you doubt this at all), and that's a direct path to back problems. Try to keep your back as straight as possible – not stiffly at attention but comfortably straight. I know of one classical guitarist who has to have a hot-water bottle behind him when playing onstage (hidden from public view, of course) because of back problems brought about by bad posture during his early development on the instrument. This is a good enough reason to make it a rule that you should sit on a comfortable, straight-backed chair when you practise and why (I say again) sofas are definitely out!

"In a Guitar Craft course, we might start by sitting on the floor and doing nothing for half an hour because, until we can do nothing, until we can ask our bodies to do nothing for a short time, we can't really ask our bodies to do something quite specific for a short time. Then we would move to the operation of the left and right hands.

If you're going to practise for four or eight hours a day, a fairly important factor is 'Can I sit on this chair for four hours?' Not 'What do I do with my guitar on this chair for four hours?' but 'Can I sit on this chair for four hours?'. So we begin by sitting on the chair or floor and doing nothing for half an hour and then we move onto 'Can I sit on a chair for three or four hours?' or whatever, because you're not going to stand and practise."
Robert Fripp

Obviously, if at any time you experience any discomfort at all in the hands, arms or whatever, for heaven's sake stop and try to work out why. Most of the time, it's down to posture, unwarranted tension, etc, and ironing out these problems now will save you a great deal of heartache in the long run. If things persist and you've done everything you can to relieve the problems yourself, you might need to seek advice from the medical profession. Quite often, it's doctors who are experienced with sports-related injuries who can provide the best advice. A lot of the problems tend to be the same – repetitive strain, tendon troubles, etc. Things can be done, although some remedies are fairly extreme, and so, as with many things in life, prevention is the best cure.

Don't Become A Hermit

"People who learn guitar tend to place the emphasis on practising alone in their rooms with a metronome rather than developing their skills by playing together with other musicians."
John Etheridge

It's tempting to take the idea of practising alone to an illogical conclusion. The guitar is a very solitary instrument and guitarists tend to be inveterate loners as a result. Violinists and cello players tend to be more gregarious because ensemble playing is the norm for them, but there are comparatively few guitar ensembles around and so guitarists tend to be moody and isolated (or is it just me?). But the benefits to be derived from playing with other musicians are manifold. Even if it's not in your personal agenda to be a part of a group, you can learn so much from playing with other

musicians that I believe it's an essential part of learning the instrument in general.

At the summer school of the International Guitar Festival held annually in Bath, we make it pretty much mandatory that all attendees perform in the student concert at the end of the week. To begin with, we have a lot of shrinking violets and people who would eat their shoes rather than play in public, but gentle cajoling from the teaching staff usually wins them over and all are unanimous that it has helped their fledgling musicianship enormously.

"I've learned a lot about how to project myself and how not to be shy, as a musician can easily be. We do spend a lot of time on our own, sitting in a corner of the room, thinking about big things, or being onstage and hiding behind our instrument. You're only confident onstage because you know you've played the tune 100,000 times at home." *Antonio Forcione*

If other musicians aren't available, then backing tracks come in as a good second best. It's good to place your playing in a different context to that of just hearing yourself unaccompanied. If no backing tracks are available, playing along to records comes in third in a three-horse race.

"I don't go through a routine of running scales or anything like that; I still like to put on an album, get the vibe and play along, or I just go over something that I need to relearn from our own material." *Robert Cray*

Good Habits Over Bad

To sum up, try to make sure that your practice time is well spent. If time is short because of the daily routine of life in general, you can still achieve wonders for your playing with a concise, well-planned-out practice routine that has progressive development built in. For instance, if you're practising scales, use a metronome and increase the speed in gentle increments once a fortnight.

Try to make everything you do have some sort of latent musical value. Instead of performing a meaningless exercise to develop right- and left-hand co-ordination, make it meaningful by ensuring that it carries with it some extra musical worth. Use an arpeggio or sing it as you play it to get some more hand-to-ear connection going, things like that. If every exercise you play has not one but several implications in this way, you're doing yourself three times as much good in the same period.

Keeping Fresh

"I'll just be sitting there and playing and then I'll come up with something by accident – a moment of inspiration." *Dominic Miller*

We all look continuously for those inspired moments when we play and something unexpected happens. We surprise ourselves by going down a path that we've perhaps left otherwise unexplored before. As for how to summon up these moments of divine inspiration, I'm afraid I can't be of much help. I've heard so many players tell me different things that it's almost impossible to draw any overall conclusions or find a common denominator. However, as long as you remain totally focused on what you're playing, these moments will get through and, like Newton's apple, perhaps take you forward a few steps in your search for your own musical identity.

"My tunes tend to evolve out of me practising. They don't really evolve out of me writing, as such, because I write a bit, I record some things, I look back at them, I update them, I lengthen them, I fix them with other bits, but there is a time when it comes together, and that was when 'Clap' came together. I could easily have called it 'Chet', because it was huge tribute to Chet Atkins. I didn't make that particularly public, but it was pretty obvious to other guitarists, despite the fact that I don't think Chet played flat-body steel-string guitar very often." *Steve Howe*

UNPLUGGED?

"I like electric guitars and so it's, like, 'Unplug this!' I won't be unplugging for anyone, thank you." Jennifer Batten, The Jeff Beck Group

This is an attempt on my part to try to sum up my reader. The chances are that you fall into one of a number of categories. You might be an electric-guitar player looking at giving your technique the necessary brush-up and general adjustment to play acoustic guitar for one or two numbers. It might be that you're new to the guitar altogether and have decided that the acoustic guitar will give you the option of playing electric guitar later on, once you've gained a bit of knowledge and dug the foundations of what will become your eventual style. You may be a hard-and-fast purist who shuns the very thought of any artificial devices like pick-ups or amplification coming between you and your art.

There will be other sub-categories and special cases, of course, but I guess that, out of the three named above, you can probably see yourself somewhere. But whatever the reason you feel drawn towards the acoustic guitar, one thing's for certain: you're either looking for an instrument to learn on or you feel that you need to upgrade to a better instrument in honour of your new-found interest. In any case, I thought I'd offer a few guidelines.

"I own one acoustic. It's a guitar I designed with Mike McGuire at Valley Arts Guitars 16 or 17 years ago. It's a one of a kind. We copied a Martin 00 but improved it with double bracing, choice of wood and so on. It's small, too." Larry Carlton

Buying An Instrument

There's no doubt that, if I'd been writing this during the 1970s or 1980s, it would be something like 10,000 words longer and most of the additional material would be words of caution. At one time, you see, it was almost impossible to buy a good acoustic guitar on a budget. Top-of-the-range handmade instruments attract top-of-the-range handmade price tags to match. We still get off fairly lightly, though – I have a friend who plays in an orchestra (he went "straight", despite intervention from me – ah well, you can't win 'em all) and he thinks nothing about buying an instrument for £25,000 and telling me that he thinks he got a bargain – so we shouldn't really moan about buying an acoustic guitar for £5,000, should we? But how many of us actually have that kind of money to invest? We want a good-quality, workmanlike instrument that feels nice to play and, most importantly, sounds great. What's more, we don't really want to part with an unnecessarily high portion of our children's inheritance in obtaining one.

"Back from the Humble Pie days, I have an Epiphone Texan which I took over to the factory and they dated it as a 1964 Sunburst, and the only other person who has one from that year and has made it famous is Paul McCartney. So he apparently recorded 'Yesterday' on an Epiphone Texan, and I did all my acoustic stuff from Humble Pie onwards – apart from one time when I used a Martin – on my Epiphone. I had it refretted and a couple of cracks sorted out over the years and it sounds better than ever." Peter Frampton

So What Costs The Money, Exactly?

I could have equally called this section, "Why Are Acoustic Guitars More Expensive Than Electric Guitars?", because that's another frequently asked question. The answer to the latter question also answers the former, and so, if I can crave your indulgence…

Building a good-quality acoustic guitar requires considerable hands-on expertise, excellent-quality materials and a lot of time and care. Even at its best, a solid-body electric guitar is a lump of wood, and most of the carving and sculpting can be done automatically on a production line. Obviously, any automated factory process is going to cut costs, but not necessarily corners; there are some superb-quality electrics out there, too.

So, given that we're talking craftsmanship here, you can begin to understand why "top of the range" can mean "second mortgage". In every area where hand carving and other similar woodworking skills are replaced by automation, there's a drop in price – and no disrespect to the manufacturers, either; there's an established market out there for good-quality, machine-built acoustics, and most manufacturers are trying their absolute darndest to fulfil customer demand. Just expect to have to compromise on a few points and you'll be fine.

I'm not painting a dark picture here, and neither am I recommending that you go down the back of the sofa looking for some extra dosh to buy something of a class and type that you're not going to need. Wait a minute, I feel some more good news coming on…

It's a fact that there are plenty of outstanding instruments in the shops these days. All are slightly different with a view to suiting the slightly different needs of the players on the market. There will definitely be one out there that will be your own best friend. Just think of me as a guy who's been around the guitar-buying block a few times and thinks he's seen it all.

So what are the points to consider? One question is going to establish two separate camps right from the start: Do you want a pure acoustic or one with a pick-up?

Just because a guitar has some means by which it can be heard through an amplifier doesn't make it an electric guitar. Many guitars now come equipped with pick-ups, and these have been dubbed "electro-acoustics". The systems by which these operate vary, but many guitars come with clever little devices that hide under the bridge and send out a signal to a cleverly disguised output hidden in the strap button. You wouldn't know it had a pick-up on board – cosmetically, at least – except that there are probably some rotary switches somewhere on the guitar's upper side that provide control over tone and volume. Other systems use internal microphones or a combination of both mic and pick-up. (See the "Performance" chapter.)

With this kind of system, your acoustic is going to have two distinct personalities: one will be its natural, acoustic voice and the other will be its electric character. In an ideal world, both would be very similar, but from a maker's perspective this is a particularly hard trick to pull off. To give a guitar a pure acoustic sound, you have to follow one particular design template: its voice is transmitted through the wood of the body, the table (the flat piece of wood on the front of the guitar) vibrates, braces within the body act together to produce different levels of bass and treble and the end result of all these different processes comes together to form a unique sonic fingerprint.

A pick-up generally takes its reference point from a single location. That is to say that, if your vibration-sensitive pick-up is located under the bridge, this is where your guitar's tone is born. Of course, everything else mentioned above can also be taken into account to determine the quality of the eventual sound, but it's still all down to that fixed point. And this is only one of the basic compromises that differentiates pure acoustic from electro-acoustic guitars.

So what's it to be? If you're unlikely to be in an actual performing or recording situation, you might be better off going for a pure acoustic. If you find yourself wanting to record at any point, there is always the tried-and-trusted process of using microphones. (In my experience, most recording engineers will mic up your acoustic irrespective of whether your guitar has an onboard pick-up. They're funny like that.) In extreme circumstances, there is the possibility to retrofit (jargon alert: this means to have something installed after purchase) a pick-up at a later date, and this fact alone ought to take care of the "don't knows" among you.

The Electro-Acoustic

It's probably fair to say that this is a more familiar animal these days than ever before. Just about every major acoustic-guitar manufacturer has an electro-acoustic range sitting alongside their truly "unplugged" variety. These guitars are great for playing at gigs, as long as you treat them right. Your average electro-acoustic is a little more temperamental than its electric brothers in that it requires either a dedicated amp or a direct feed into a PA system. It definitely won't sound too good through a normal electric-guitar amplifier.

Then there's the question of feedback. If you're not familiar with this particular audio phenomenon, then I can assume that you've never tried plugging either a guitar or a microphone into an amp, turning the volume up and standing nearby. This course of action generally results in a high-pitched squeal that's loud enough to take out both eardrums at once. Welcome to the wacky world of feedback, boys 'n' girls. I won't bore you with a full electronics thesis on why this particular fact of life exists; let's just agree that it's best avoided, especially at gigs, where it can upset a sensitive audience who were looking forward to an evening of gentle acoustic music.

Electro-acoustic guitars are, you see, prone to feedback if not handled carefully and respectfully. To avoid it completely, you need the reflexes of a cat and a quick-witted sound engineer.

So, given that the electro-enhanced acoustic guitar can take on the characteristics of a screaming banshee at the drop of a hat, what exactly are the upsides to the situation? For a start, you don't have to stand statue-still in front of a microphone onstage fearing that a simple gesture left or right with the guitar will affect the sound quality. Secondly, and probably more importantly, you can usually rely on getting a more consistent sound from gig to gig. This is because the guitar and its electronics have been designed around each other to produce the best possible results. So, as a package deal, you can expect this marriage made in acoustic-guitar heaven to be easier to handle live. Plus, of course, you have a set of controls on your guitar that at least gives you some sort of feeling that you're actually in control – or at least as much as

anyone can be in control in the somewhat hostile acoustic environment of a pub or club.

Any more downsides to consider? Well, like I said, if you're building an electro-acoustic model, you're really trying to build two guitars in one. Ideally, you want a good acoustic sound and a good electronic representation of that exact same sound, right? Unfortunately, in the same way that there's no such thing as a perfect world, there's almost no chance of pulling this one off 100 per cent of the time, either. If I was going to generalise, I would say that budget acoustic guitars are lacking in the bass department. This is due to the fact that the sheer craftsmanship required in the building process that gives both volume and a good bass response calls for more hands-on attention to detail than a machine-based assembly line can really be expected to achieve.

So we can't expect too much natural bass at the budget end. What's more, a guitar that is built to perform well in the electric field will come up a little tonally short in the acoustic arena. It's just a fact of life. But you, as a discerning guitar buyer (which you will be by the end of this chapter), can at least expect the best possible compromise.

The answer, as always, is to listen to the guitar and compare it to others in your chosen price range. If possible, take a friend with you who can play the guitar and will let you listen, vice versa or both. The nature of acoustics is that they sound different about six feet away from how they do when you are literally on top of them. Also, it goes without saying that you should explore both the acoustic and electric virtues of your would-be purchase before making a decision.

Pure Acoustics

"The pure acoustic that I use the most is my Taylor." *Steve Vai*

Most of what I've already said applies to acoustics without any onboard electronic gubbins, of course. Here you can afford to concentrate on the instrument's pure tone, and listening well at point of purchase is vital. Forget the sales talk that might offer to throw in a tutorial book and a plectrum and instead concentrate on the look, feel and tone of what you're holding in your hands.

Body Wood

Acoustic connoisseurs have certain expectations from an instrument that are based more on its individual parts than on its overall appearance and tonal qualities. In the main, these tend to orbit around which woods have been used in manufacture. Amongst the good woods that you might expect to find on a new guitar's manifest, you might see the following:

Spruce
Cedar
Ebony
Rosewood
Mahogany
Maple

This list is far from exhaustive, but it probably represents the body-wood mainstream. Beware of expressions like "laminated pine", however; this translates to "plywood" once the outrageous sales hyperbole has been scraped away. Although, you know, it's interesting to note that the Gibson ES175 – the default jazz guitar for many wonderful professionals – has a top made from plywood and yet its tone is absolutely spot on, as far as electric jazz is concerned. Still, mention this guitar to many luthiers and they will run for the garlic and sharp stakes, insisting that such a wood is the work of the Dark One. It just goes to show that the quirk factor is alive and well in guitar manufacture, too.

The next thing to consider is whether you go for a solid top or a laminate, the "top" being the face of the guitar, as opposed to the back, sides, neck or fingerboard. The difference is a fairly obvious one, from a purely technical point of view: one is solid wood, the other is a nice-looking piece of wood glued onto not such a nice piece. The former tends to represent expensive guitars while the latter is produced for the more budget-conscious. Of course, you just know I'm going to say that this isn't always the case, don't you? Sure enough, I've played some laminated tops that were absolutely sublime and some solid-tops that were total dogs. Paradoxically, whereas laminated tops are definitely a "budget" feature, they tend to be stronger than solid-tops in some cases. But I'm not going to attempt a treatise on wood types and all the various processes involved in luthiery. All I can say is that I'm trying to offer a general guide here. If in doubt, ten minutes with a luthier or expert repairer will set you straight.

"In California in the early '70s, I came across an old Martin D28 with a small crack in it. The guy wanted very little money for it because he didn't know what he had, and so I took it in a flash. I took it to a guitar repairer and had it fixed up and I've still got it now.

"I've got my own signature model through Brook Guitars in Devon. Basically, it's a 0028-sized D28. It's got a spruce top, ebony fingerboard, mahogany neck, rosewood sides and back. The neck is very simple – the only position marker is at the twelfth fret, where there is a white rose with 'TR' on it. It's very stylish." *Tim Rose*

Inside Story

"My main guitar is still a Levin acoustic jumbo. It's about 30 years old. I also have a wonderful Gibson J45, which is what you hear on the solo stuff." *Eric Bibb*

While you're inspecting the outside of a guitar, don't forget the insides, too. One dead giveaway of shoddy workmanship is huge dollops of glue everywhere inside – on the bracing and the shaped wood around the edges that has been "notched" to fit around the contours. (We call this process *kerfing*, if you're interested.) A good furniture maker would never be so untidy, and you've a perfect right to expect neatness here, too. Of course, you can't look everywhere inside without going into the shop equipped with a torch and an engineer's mirror (a rather natty idea of having a mirror on the end of a flexible cable to allow you to look around corners), but this simple rule of thumb will be another item you can tick off your quality checklist.

You might be wondering how you tell a solid top from a laminated one – yes? To be honest, it's probably something that you'll have to ask the salesman (dodgy, I know, but some of 'em know what they're talking about), or you may have to check the spec in a catalogue or magazine review.

One thing you can do is look at the wood that has been used for the top of the guitar. Does it look as though it's quality wood? Is the grain straight? Does what you're holding in your hands look like a piece of quality workmanship or a box of bits thrown together in a sweatshop somewhere? Trust your instincts on this one.

What's the balance like? If you sit down with the guitar, is it neck-heavy, body-heavy, or do you feel that, if you let go, it would just remain on your lap like a faithful puppy?

Another thing to look at, apart from general build quality, is hardware. Do the tuners (or tuning pegs) look cheap and plastic? I don't have to point out that a guitar with cheapo tuners probably isn't going to stay in tune for very long. And if there's an obvious quality compromise here, you're likely to find it everywhere else on the instrument. What about the nut? (This is the bit the strings pass over at the top of the neck, just below the tuners.) Do the slots that have been cut for the strings look neat? Is the nut plastic (not always great) or bone (a sure sign of quality)? Believe it or not, there's a composite on the market that has the basic weight and feel of bone but is in fact synthetic. You'll probably have to resort to asking or checking the written spec on this issue, too. It's darned hard to tell them apart, sometimes.

Take a look down the neck from the tuner end. Are the frets even, or do you get the general impression that you're looking at a hillside graveyard? If everything looks straight and the frets themselves look uniformly round and polished, there's a better chance that all is well in this department, too. Frets aren't always what they seem, and it certainly isn't true that a fret is a fret and that there's little difference from one type to the next. Cheap fretwire is about as sturdy and hardwearing as cucumber and you'll find little pits and grooves appearing with comparatively little use. It's difficult to tell the good stuff from the cheap stuff. Once again, you have to consider overall build quality. Is it really likely that, on a guitar with cheapo plastic tuners and a plywood top, you'll find expensive, hardwearing fretwire? Also, if the frets look like they've

spent a few years at sea, having become dulled and tarnished and generally weary of life, suspect that not all is well and try to get a second opinion.

A good guitar teacher will gladly accompany you to buy a new instrument, especially if you're a little unsure of all the various pitfalls that could snag the unwary. I used to do this all the time, mainly because it was in my interests as well as my students' to make sure that they got good instruments. Teaching someone to play is hard enough, but the job becomes 300 per cent harder if the student is constantly having to fight with his instrument.

"I got a Gibson. I was told that it was called the Sailor model, like a J100 size. It had a hole punched in the top. It was not a great guitar, but it was just what I needed to get started. Then I got a Gibson J45 in 1961 and that was the guitar I used until I got a J200 in 1963, but the neck warped the wrong way and I couldn't get it fixed. I was in a guitar store in New York and they had a 1947 Gibson Country & Western that had been owned by Josh Graves. I got it for 400 bucks and I played that guitar for 20 years." *John Hammond*

Guitar-Shopping Checklist

I've constructed a list of points below to look for when buying either an electro-acoustic or a pure acoustic.

- Solid top or laminate?
- Do the tuners look cheap?
- Do the frets look neat, even and polished?
- Are the insides neat and tidy?
- Is it made of a quality bodywood?
- Is it balanced?
- Does the nut look neatly cut?
- Finally, but most importantly, does it sound any good?

A good guitar shop will generally have a "quiet room" in which customers can play an acoustic guitar unhindered by the endless renditions of 'Smoke On The Water' in the establishment's main area. If there isn't such a facility, it might mean that the shop doesn't really care whether you buy a good or bad instrument. Just leave. It's the only way they'll learn.

Strings

It's true enough that guitarists are well known for discussing their strings in earnest little huddles. Sometimes, it's the only exciting thing that they ever get to do, apart from waxing lyrical about exactly which version of Davy Graham's 'Anji' they're learning. But it's true that the subject isn't generally addressed in guitar tutors and, seeing as it's an important one, do me a favour and settle yourself down with a mug of coffee and a pack of biscuits and indulge an old man for a paragraph or two.

The reason why I consider the subject of strings to be so important is this: strings play a vital role in your tonal output. Plus, they're relatively cheap and there's a very confusing variety available on the market. Back in the Dark Ages, I used to work in a guitar shop and I was constantly amazed by the number of people who would come in and ask for a set of guitar strings, and when I enquired what sort, I was met with a sort of weak "I dunno" type of grin. Let's get one thing straight: strings are important. So let's form a little huddle while we talk the subject through.

If you're coming over to acoustic guitar having played electric for a long time, one of the first things you need to make yourself aware of is the fact that acoustic string gauges are generally heavier than their electric counterparts. Why? The answer is rooted in physics, once again, but not the type of physics that puts any undue strain on the average guitarist, fear not. On an electric guitar, you rely on electromagnetics to produce a sound. The electric guitar has a fairly feeble acoustic voice – although it's an important component here, too – but the pick-ups soon compensate for this, producing electronic volume levels of anything from "aah" to "ouch" and beyond. It's a fairly well-known fact that you can get more response from the string of an electric guitar by increasing the thickness, as more metal vibrating in the pick-up's magnetic field produces a higher current for the amplifier to chew on and spew out. Guitarists who have experimented will agree that they seem to get an improvement in general tone, too. Roughly speaking, more metal also transfers nuances

such as vibrato more faithfully. And this is where the similarity crosses over to acoustic.

An acoustic guitar generally relies on the vibration of body woods, bracing and so on to produce tone. If you fit your guitar with strings that are too thin (ie .009 gauge), your tone and volume will be impaired.

Case History

I had a pupil called Mel who was into acoustic blues. She bought herself a nice instrument that was part of a very famous manufacturer's range and everything was set to turn her into one of the Essex Delta's finest – except that she wasn't happy with the tone of her guitar at all. She had a sound in her head that the guitar simply couldn't reproduce. I asked her to bring in some recordings of guitars with the tone she was shooting for and she came the next week with an armful of cassettes. I listened to a variety of artists like Robert Johnson, the Reverend Gary Davis, Son House and so on, picked up her guitar and played a stylised approximation of what I'd heard. She agreed that we'd got most of the notes right but noted that the tone was still lacking. I suggested that she should experiment with strings, and that she should go with a fairly expensive brand to make sure that the guitar had the optimum opportunity to be heard at its best. Mel still wasn't happy. I said I thought it sounded nice and rich and probably about as good as she was going to get without spending thousands on a top-class instrument, but she said that the sound was too good – too rich and not at all like the sounds that she was hearing on her favourite Delta blues albums. I finally twigged that, whereas I had been making allowances for the fact that the recordings we were listening to were in some cases the result of early-20th-century recording techniques (primitive at best), she hadn't. She actually wanted her guitar to sound thin and, dare I say it, tinny. I pointed this out, but there was no arguing with her. Her guitar sounded too good. So I suggested that she should go out and buy a set of electric guitar strings and put them on, as this is probably the worst thing you can do to an acoustic guitar, tonally speaking. She did so, came in next week and the guitar sounded reedy and thin. I despaired. Mel was ecstatic. (Hey, the customer is always right, OK?)

Gauges

"I use an 11-52 string gauge [on both electric and acoustic guitars]. I can pretty much play my Martin the same way I can play an electric guitar. I can bend the twelve up a minor third pretty easily. I don't have any problem, as I've pretty strong fingers." *Robbie McIntosh*

If you've ever walked into a guitar shop and asked for a packet of strings, you'll be aware of the somewhat dizzying amount of variety on offer. We've already seen that, unless your name's Mel, you'll be steering clear of electric-guitar strings, and so that's already some help in finding your way through this particular maze. What's left to you is a range of different manufacturers' product, all in very similar-looking packs. But how do you tell which is the best for you? Well, I'm going to tell you a little secret. If you're not the type that enjoys gossip, you can avoid reading the next paragraph, but if you want to avoid in-store option anxiety, read on.

There are loads of different makes of string on the market, but there are only a few string manufacturers on the planet – that is, factories that turn wire into guitar strings – so you have the case where a few manufacturing plants make strings for just about everyone. In other words, sometimes there's very little actual difference between makes of string. Your best bet is to experiment, as far as makes are concerned, and leave all your decision-making expertise for deciding which gauge you're going to use.

As far as actual gauge is concerned, the rule is "the thicker, the better" for all of the reasons relating to tone and volume I've covered above. This translates into "the heaviest set that you can feasibly work with". Don't be afraid of being thought a wimp if a set of elevens feels right – that's fine. I wouldn't recommend that you aim any lower, though, as you'll be in danger of quickly getting into the thin-and-reedy arena that Mel liked so much.

As a guide, I'd say that a set of twelves might be a good choice to start with. In this way, you can defer to elevens if they feel too heavy or progress up to 13s if you've been working out at the gym.

The individual gauges within a set of strings will vary slightly from manufacturer to manufacturer. Here are two examples:

	Set A	Set B
E	.012	.012
B	.016	.016
G	.025	.024
D	.032	.032
A	.042	.042
E	.054	.053

Not a great deal of difference, is there? And I drew both sets from my own personal swag bag (guess which gauge I use?) pretty much at random. You might be surprised (or, if you're making the jump to acoustic after years of playing electric guitar, quite shocked) to learn that twelves are considered to be only a light gauge by both manufacturers concerned.

Like I've said, experimentation is really the only way forward with strings. You'll almost certainly find one particular gauge and brand that suits your needs as a guitarist. When you do, stick with it.

"The nylon-string acoustic is made by a guy called Rubio. It's basically a top-of-the-line student model which my wife bought me for my birthday a couple of years ago. It was fun to be able to use that... It's a real good guitar. The steel-string which I used on 'Nothin' To Nobody' and 'Water For The Wicked' is a Guild D40, a kind of a small-bodied, great guitar. I've used it on just about everything I've recorded that calls for a six-string acoustic and I borrow it from a friend of mine." *Robben Ford*

Nylon-String Guitars

"I received two guitars at the same time. They had been made together. One was slightly better and slightly different to the other, and I preferred it. The maker couldn't understand why and went back over his notes. The only thing he could come up with was that the polystyrene he had used to protect the wood while he pressed together the cedar and carbon fibre had been of a different density!" *John Williams*

Throughout this book, I'm concentrating mainly on the steel-strung type of acoustic guitar and not deviating into, say, arch-top jazzers or semi-acoustic electrics. I wasn't going to talk too much about nylon-string guitars, either, but there is a new breed of nylon-string guitars (and players) around who have managed to coax this quietly voiced breed of instrument along to the party going on in contemporary music.

You don't need me to tell you that most classical guitars are made with one purpose in mind: the playing of classical guitar music. Obviously, classical guitar is a completely different discipline when it comes to studying. Virtually everything to do with learning classical guitar is different from learning the more popular styles – position, repertoire, fingering and so on – and the decision whether or not to learn to read music is made for you; you've no choice but to learn, it's really that simple. So it stands to reason that there are whole shelves full of classical tutors written with the instrument's indigenous characteristics solely to the fore. We can learn a lot from some of the right-hand fingering techniques, but we don't need to make the whole journey; we can get off at one of the earlier stops *en route*. The difference between the two music disciplines is a little like the difference between professional ballet and jogging around at the local disco, but a number of players have taken the nylon-string guitar and used it as an effective voice within the context of rock, jazz, new age, pop or whatever, and so this instrument deserves its own space in this book.

I suppose that one of the things that kept the classical guitar off the modern music stage was volume. As a breed, they're fairly modestly voiced beasts – unless, that is, you're going for top-of-the-line concert models, which are completely different animals altogether and much louder. But thanks to the under-saddle pick-up revolution, nylon-string guitars can now find a voice courtesy of a PA system. Nearly all of these models carry their own onboard volume and tone controls (like their steel-string cousins) and therefore can go the distance onstage.

A couple of manufacturers have brought out models that are essentially solid-body instruments and yet still retain the sonic characteristics of the full-acoustic versions. Once again, this is thanks to piezo-fired under-saddle pick-ups.

If you've found yourself seduced by the nylon-string guitar's arguably more romantic tonal palette, there are plenty of models to choose from. Most of what I said above holds fast for the classical variety of guitar – solid-top versus laminate, good-quality woods, hardware and so on are all-important concerns here, too – but once again ease of playing and overall sound quality should be your main priorities and, once again, a second opinion should be sought if you're at all unsure of anything concerning a potential purchase.

"I've got three Yairis. I've been using them for about 20 years. I use one to record with which has a beautiful depth to it, while the other two I use for live work. They have the advantage of having a cutaway and are very evenly balanced. They are very bright, but each string is the same volume. If you are using them live with a desk out front, you have to use subtractive EQ to roll off some of the top end and mellow it slightly. They are purely acoustic and so I don't have to mess around with batteries." *Steve Hackett*

Strings

A word of caution here: classical guitar strings are made from nylon (at least, the top three strings are; the rest are metal-wrapped around either nylon strands or silk) and nylon stretches like mad when you first bring a string up to tension. This results in the string going madly out of tune until it reaches that happy equilibrium where it's got its stretching out of its system and is quite happy to sit there and stay in tune. Cheaper classical-guitar strings go out of tune more – or so my own personal experience has taught me, at any rate. Be prepared to fork out for a quite expensive string if you want a relatively stress-free tuning experience. They won't break the bank and they'll keep you out of therapy for a while longer.

Ear Training

"I leave more to the imagination of the listener, you know, instead of saying, 'OK, this is the colour you should be seeing now.' It's like if you're reading a really good book – you imagine who the antagonist is and you imagine who the protagonist is." *Vernon Reid*

It might be tempting to think that the only thing you've got to get in tune is your guitar, but this simply isn't the case. By far the most important thing to get in tune is you, and this is a thing that is sadly so often ignored when anyone takes up a musical instrument.

It's certainly a common error to believe that music begins with a pick stroke or a fretted note. It doesn't. Music should start with you first hearing the note in your head. Now, I know that a lot of people at seminars start shifting uncomfortably in their seats whenever I mention this fact, but it's absolutely true, and I think I can prove it.

If I asked you to pick up your guitar and play the first thing that came into your head, what would you play? My guess would be that you'd play something you already knew how to play – you almost certainly wouldn't take the risk of improvising a line out of nowhere. But I bet you wish you could. What's more, you don't need me to tell you how, because it's something you know how to do already.

If I asked you to talk about a random subject for 30 seconds, you'd probably be able to, especially if it was a subject that you knew a lot about. Let's say I asked you to talk about your favourite holiday or a nice restaurant you've discovered. In this case, you might even find that 30 seconds wasn't long enough! But if I asked you to do the same thing again, this time musically, what would be the problem? I could give you the equivalent of a subject ("Play me something in E major for 30 seconds") or something more abstract ("Play me something that reminds you of the sea"), but most of the time students don't really know where to begin.

I believe that there are a great many comparisons to be made between language and music. In fact, as far as I'm concerned music *is* a language and, in a lot of ways, can be taught as such.

Let's examine exactly what was going on when you spent 30 seconds telling me about your 18-30 holiday in Ibiza (or weekend in Clacton). The things you'd have called upon were, very basically, your knowledge of the language and your memories of the event itself. You would probably have been able to talk fairly continuously and what you said would have made coherent sense, and yet you probably wouldn't have been exactly conscious of where the words, thoughts and ideas were coming from. You wouldn't have literally "heard" everything you said just before you said it, and so we can assume that what you were doing was in fact improvising on a theme. You weren't reading from a script, and if I asked you to tell the story again five minutes later you wouldn't do it in exactly the same way that you told it originally.

We can reach that same level musically, too. When a musician claims that he plays spontaneously and that he doesn't actually have to think about what he's doing, I believe he's using the exact same set of instincts and responses. And yet we've already agreed that all that was happening when you gave your talk was that you were calling on some things you'd taken for granted since you were a child: language and memory.

So how does this translate into learning music? Can we ever really reach the level where we're as confident, natural and informed about music as we are about the fundamentals of language? I believe it can be done and that the job begins with the all-important task of ear training.

Adjust Your Listening Habits

"I gave up ruining records trying to work out every note Robert Johnson played, but during the years all of this listening has really started to come back into the writing. I think basically that that's the way to go." *Eric Bibb*

Just as we begin to learn the basics of language merely by being surrounded by people who are ready and willing to talk to us as infants, a lot of the initial spadework concerning learning the language of music comes from listening. The thing is, you might have to adjust slightly your ideas about listening to music.

Many people spend a few hours every day listening to music, but mainly as background noise – in the car, in the supermarket or on the radio at home, for instance. Taken on such a superficial level, this might be a fine way of keeping yourself amused, but it's not going to input anything too useful into your brain, musically speaking. What you need to set about is a course of action whereby you listen to material that will be of benefit to you and give it your entire concentration when you do.

Joe Pass used to recommend that listening should be as much a part of your practice routine as playing scales or working on a new piece of music, so make time to listen to music that inspires you. Buy a decent pair of headphones or a personal hi-fi, shut off the rest of the world and just listen.

Many players say that, by doing this, they've absorbed music unconsciously and have learned a lot about music's more subtle areas of technique, such as phrasing, tone, dynamics and so on. Try to put yourself in a receptive state of mind when you listen to music. To achieve the best results, the mind has to enter an almost meditative state. Only then will the music enter your brain on a level that will permeate your unconscious and take up residence as part of your musical nature.

Incidentally, if all this sounds a little kung-fu, I apologise (Grasshopper), but it really does have an effect.

Open Your Mind

We've all got our prejudices, as far as music is concerned. We all shut out certain styles or artists in preference to listening to a narrow band of material of our own choosing. One thing I used to make sure of when I taught was that I introduced my students to guitarists that they hadn't heard of, asking them to park their prejudice at the door when they came in. Often, they would discover new influences from areas of playing that they'd never previously suspected would do them any good. I've spoken to a good many hard rock guitarists who said they learned a lot of new tricks by listening to country music, for example.

A good and thoroughly modern way of finding out what's hot and what's not on the guitar front is by eavesdropping on one of the many Internet news groups dedicated to the guitar. (And if you want any examples of blind prejudice in music, look no further!) Here you will see the names of many players and artists who are unfamiliar to you, and you may just strike gold by checking out a few of them.

Get Out More

"I was too shy to ask anyone to show me anything. I just watched real well when they played. But seeing how important the song was… I mean, I found that the guitar enhanced the song, as opposed to taking it over, so I tried really hard not to overplay notes that weren't necessary. If it supported the words and made the song clearer, then I felt that was more important." *John Hammond*

There is enormous benefit to be had from going out to see live music, too. Watching various performers can give you all sorts of new ideas that you can go home and work on. Every so often, you'll find yourself in a situation where you see someone play something you've been trying to work out for ages and it could just provide you with that final nugget of information you need to complete the puzzle.

Once again, I'd recommend that you adopt as broad-minded an attitude as possible when seeking out live music. I've certainly found myself in the position where I've found myself at a concert and someone I've not previously heard of has amazed and inspired me.

Don't be afraid to ask questions, either. When pressed, most guitarists I know love to talk about playing (sometimes it's the only chance they get) and will freely answer any questions about technique, style or whatever. Think of it as research – you need as much input as possible in order to make your own analysis and draw your own conclusions, and it's these elements that will fuse together and start to form your style.

Ear Training II

Of course, it's not all putting your feet up and listening to music and then going down to the nearest pub staging live music for a night out; there's some work to be done in the practice room, too. As far as tips in this area are concerned, I'd ask you to consider the following…

- Tune your guitar by ear. If you use an electronic tuner, you don't need to use it every time. Try tuning it unaided occasionally and bring the tuner in at the end to hear what kind of a job you've made of things. By all means tune one string to the tuner first, however, just to make sure that the rest of the strings are tuned to a relative pitch.

- Buy an A440 pitchfork (no, not the farm implement) and carry it around with you. From time to time, take it out and listen to it. After a while, you might find that you're beginning to recognise the pitch of A in the music you listen to. Certainly, you might find yourself able to anticipate the pitch before you listen to the fork.

- Sing everything you play. This is one for the practice area. If you're playing an exercise or working on a tune, try singing or humming along as you play. This is one of the most important steps towards tying together the music in your head and what you're doing with your hands.

- Expose your ear to as much as you can. Buy a scale book, play through what you find inside, listen to the sound made by different combinations of notes and assess whether they might be useful to you in your music.

- Do the exercise on the CD (which we'll come to later).

You Sing It, I'll Play It

What we're working towards here is enabling you to play anything you hear in your head. If the music's not in your head, you can't be expected to play it unless it's written down for you first. I feel a case history coming on…

Case History

I had a pupil who was trying to work out a solo on a record and he desperately wanted to do it by himself, without my help. However, he was obviously having problems, because he came to me for a few tips. (He didn't want me to work it out for him; he was set on doing it for himself.) I asked him to play me what he'd already worked out and he'd got it about 96 per cent nailed, it was just this troublesome passage in the middle that he couldn't quite get his ears around, so I asked him to hum it for me. He was quite taken aback, but as he was used to me taking a somewhat askance view on teaching guitar, he tried it. He didn't even get close. I asked him why he thought this was and he said that he didn't know.

I worked out the troublesome passage for him and told him exactly why he was having trouble with it. It was simply that the vocabulary of the phrase in question hadn't cropped up in his experience before. It was like he'd come across an unfamiliar word, had a stab at pronouncing it and got it wildly off the mark. His ear simply hadn't been introduced to this particular combination of notes before, and so he had no basis on which to work. I showed him a scale (I think it was a harmonic minor) in which this particular arrangement of notes lived quite happily, and he saw it instantly. He had no trouble actually playing the passage because, with his technique, he was more than capable of doing so. He merely lacked some of the ear-training skills necessary to wheedle it out of a recording.

This brings me around to my next topic, which is determining for yourself what your musical problems are and how to take steps to cure them.

Musical Or Physical?

In my experience, all problems on the guitar can be assigned to one of two principal causes: they're nearly always either musical or physical problems.

My pupil in the case history above had a musical problem: he could play the phrase in question but couldn't hear it in his head. If it had been the other way around, the problem would have been physical and could have been addressed by exercises to develop the area in which he was having problems. See how it works?

In general, all musical problems can be solved by ear training and all physical problems can be solved with practice. All you have to do is be very specific when diagnosing the symptoms so that the solutions you put in place hit the mark with the utmost precision.

A healthy practice routine should address both sides of your musical development, in any case, but there is bound to be the occasional imbalance. In general, ear training is ignored in favour of pumping iron in the guitar gym, and this will get you by because nothing will be beyond your physical reach as a musician, but I can generally detect the fretboard gymnasts because they tend to resort to playing patterns (repetitive finger movements) and everything sounds "worked out" instead of natural and musical. So you can take great steps towards enhancing your own musical wellbeing by taking some time to develop your ear.

You've probably guessed by now that I'm going to say that a lot of the problems I've encountered with students tend to fall on the side of musical problems rather than physical ones, and you're right, I am. This is maybe because ear training is such a subtle process and because the benefits take a while to become evident. What's more, progress in ear training is difficult to measure – you can tell if you can play a scale or an exercise faster than you did three weeks ago, but how can you tell that your ear has improved?

So, if you've ever had private lessons and wondered why your teacher has spent an inordinate amount of time training your ear, now you know why. Here's another case history to mull over...

Case History

I had a pupil who (quite rightly) wanted to work out some guitar parts for himself but was becoming frustrated when he found that he just couldn't seem to nail them accurately enough. I knew right away that his ear wasn't sufficiently developed, so I told him about the Personal Everest syndrome and advised him that he was trying to work out material that was still out of reach. I suggested that he try to work on far simpler stuff and be disciplined enough to stick at it without allowing himself to think that he was in any way displaying any shortcomings, musically speaking. He was patient enough to follow my advice, and before too long his ear was picking up things that had eluded him before. Patient, persistent practice paid off again!

If you want to be able to listen to a piece of music – a guitar solo, a melody line or whatever – and work it out for yourself, you have to follow the advice above and start with simple tunes that you know well. I suggest nursery rhymes, tunes that have been with you since you were very young and have been engraved on your consciousness. However, whatever music you choose, the process is nearly always the same:

- Tackle the tune in short bursts, say, four notes at a time.

- Listen, hum and play. Don't miss out the humming stage, because this is important – it places the music inside your head and is also a good way of building up your perceptive skills.

- Be patient and remember that you're working on something that needs time to develop. Nothing comes overnight.

Another good idea (which I believe I stole from Herb Ellis) is to play a tune you know from a note selected at random on the fretboard – literally, just plonk your finger down on a note and try to play your selected tune from there. And keep it simple – once again, a nursery rhyme is ideal. This is an invaluable exercise, because it really begins to firm up your orientation skills on the fretboard. Also, realising the best place on the fretboard to play a melody or a tune fragment does wonders for your sense of phrasing.

Occasionally, tell yourself that you'll work out your tune solely on a single pair of strings – G and D, for instance. By doing this, you're forced into thinking about the fretboard from a "horizontal" point of view.

All of these exercises prepare you for life out in the real musical world and will build up your confidence and knowledge of your instrument.

Let's Get Physical

As for the other side of things, physical problems, I've said already that these have to be addressed by practising, but you've also got to be able to determine exactly how to practise the things that are getting in the way of your playing. Knowing the problem is only halfway towards determining a solution.

You have to ask yourself questions like "Is this problem a general one? Does it crop up in other pieces I'm trying to play?" If you do this, you might be able to sort out a few problems at once. As an example, you might be trying to learn a specific piece and find that there's a fast passage in it that always trips you up – that, no matter how often you practise the piece, it's always there, lying in wait. The question to ask here is "Do I have problems with other fast passages? Do I need to work on my speed?" If so, hammering away at some scales with a metronome is going to begin to address the problem nicely.

Other problems might be more specific. There might be a phrase with an awkward fingering that always gives you a hard time. Ask yourself "Is there another way that I can play this phrase while avoiding that cruel fingering? Could I modify the fingering and make it easier by playing the phrase at a different place on the guitar neck?" It's the ability to diagnose and solve your own problems that will guarantee faster progress on the guitar. Don't live with them; solve them!

Another tip to add here is that you should always isolate any problematic areas within a piece and practise them separately. Imagine you had a list of three or four problem phrases; keep a note of all of them and spend some time playing through each of them slowly and methodically before you do anything else. This is quite often a great method of "defusing" a problem and rendering it harmless. One of the reasons why these musical S-bends continue to bother us for an eternity is that we build up a psychological attitude to them that tells us they'll never really be solved. This has the effect that you see the trouble-spot looming ahead when you're playing through the rest of the piece and then, by the time you've reached it, you're in the wrong state of mind to deal with it. It's reached the level of a phobia and so, sick with your continuing failure, you plod on, convinced there's no end in sight to your shortcomings. I'm not painting a pretty picture here, but I bet it's one that sounds uncannily familiar to you.

This is where tackling your problems in isolation will pay off. Tell yourself that everyone has been through what you're going through. We've all had our screaming fits when we can't manage something first, second or 35th time, but it's those of us who exorcise our demons by separating off the problem concerned and dealing with it separately who have long since stopped sleeping with the light on.

The CD Exercise

On the CD provided, you'll find an ear-training game that I used to play with my pupils. As far as ear training is concerned, the ability to recognise a pitch and hum it is really only half the story. You'll also need to be able to find the note on your guitar. Otherwise, the job's only half done.

You don't need me to tell you that the guitar is tuned in such a way that quite a few notes tend to repeat all over the place. For instance, you'll perhaps already be aware that the note C that can be found on the first fret on your B string can also be found on the fifth fret on the G string, the tenth fret on the D, the 15th fret on the A and, if your fretboard extends far enough, on the 20th fret on the bottom E string. That's five versions of the same note. Because of this fact, it's sometimes difficult to visualise the question of pitch on the guitar. It's easy on a piano – you start on the left with all the low notes and finish on the far right with all the high ones. Nothing too controversial there. But the guitar's different, and so it's definitely a good idea to acclimatise yourself to its somewhat surreal pitching.

For a start, it's not helpful to have a visual idea of how the guitar encompasses its musical range like this:

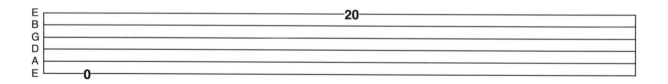

It's actually more appropriate to have a mental picture of it that looks more like this:

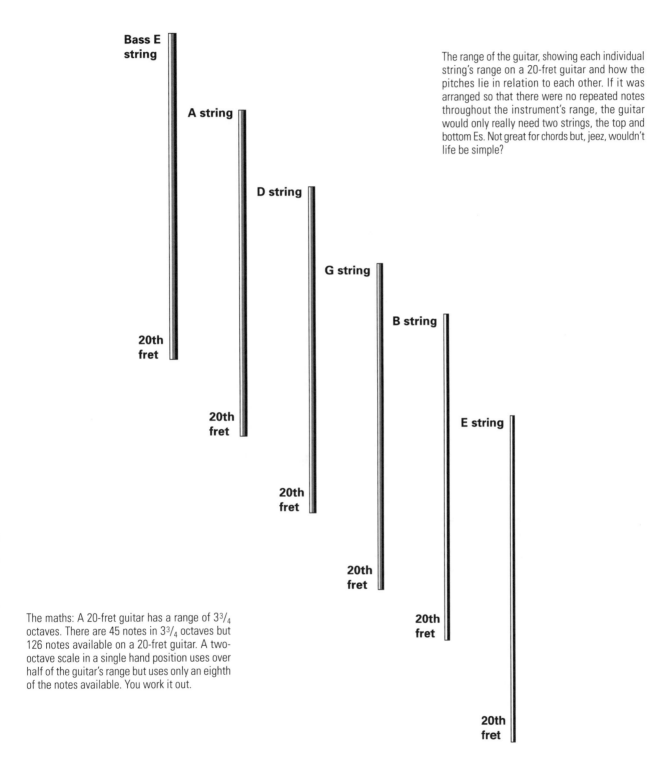

The range of the guitar, showing each individual string's range on a 20-fret guitar and how the pitches lie in relation to each other. If it was arranged so that there were no repeated notes throughout the instrument's range, the guitar would only really need two strings, the top and bottom Es. Not great for chords but, jeez, wouldn't life be simple?

The maths: A 20-fret guitar has a range of $3^3/_4$ octaves. There are 45 notes in $3^3/_4$ octaves but 126 notes available on a 20-fret guitar. A two-octave scale in a single hand position uses over half of the guitar's range but uses only an eighth of the notes available. You work it out.

Here, it's easier to see exactly how many notes on the guitar fretboard are unique (ie notes that you can't play anywhere else) and which ones are represented all over the place.

A couple more facts and figures should emphasise this mental image that we're building nicely. For instance, a piano has a range of about eight octaves, a saxophone has two and a bit and the guitar has between three and four, depending on how many frets you have. Acoustic guitars normally have around 20 frets, but this varies according to make and age (ie older guitars can have fewer). A 20-fret guitar would have a range of three and two-thirds of an octave. This means that, if you were to play the scale shown here…

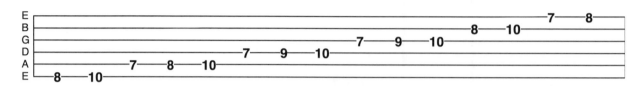

…you'd be using more than half of the guitar's range from a single position. This might give you a better idea of what we're up against when considering the question of playing a specific pitch. In classical guitar, the question of where you play a note is almost as important as how it's played. Fingering is everything, for both left and right hands, and classical players can pore over music for ages just working out the logistics of how it can be played both economically and, most importantly, musically.

What all of this is leading up to is a game of fretboard orienteering. It's simple: I play a note, having given you some *big* clues as to its approximate location on the fretboard; you (hum it and) find it. As we progress, the clues get more sparse – I increase the area in which the note can be found and you have to call on more of your musical instincts.

A lot of the pupils I tried this exercise with were surprised at how accurate they could become, and the knock-on effect was that they could best guess the location of a guitar note when they heard it. Now, there's a handy thing to develop when you're working out guitar parts from records!

So, on the CD, we start off on a single string, between the first and twelfth frets. I play one note at a time, you hum it to yourself and find its location on the string. Then I'll play some notes that are on pairs of strings, then sets of strings and so on.

I'm not handing out any answers, either, and before you accuse me of being a cruel and terrible person, here's why: whenever I do something like this and the answers are in the back of the book, I cheat. Another reason is that there are so many notes you've got to find that you can play the game any number of times before you start to remember where the notes are.

So fetch your guitar, pop on the CD and play the game of fretboard orienteering. I realise that it's not going to challenge Monopoly or Scrabble in terms of either longevity or downhome family fun, but it's going to be of great benefit to you.

On The CD

- Notes on the A string between the first and twelfth frets.

- Notes on the B string between the first and twelfth frets.

- Notes on the D string between the first and twelfth frets.

- Notes on the G and B strings.

- Notes on the A and D strings.

- Notes on the G, B and E strings.

- Notes on all six strings.

TUNING

There are many ways to tune a guitar, but I'd advise you to buy an electronic tuner to begin with. Guitars go out of tune with frustrating regularity, and if your ears aren't yet quite up to speed then you'll need to check the tuning every time you sit down to practise or play. There really isn't anything worse than listening to an out-of-tune instrument and there are few things worse for you than trying to practise on a guitar that needs a few tweaks in the tuning department, either.

Your ability to tune your guitar accurately will develop as time goes by, but initially you're going to need some help, and so purchasing an electronic aid is going to help you a lot. There is a wide range of models on the market, but if your guitar doesn't have any onboard electronics then you should make sure you buy one that has a built-in microphone or it will be of little use to you. Tuning should be carried out in peace and quiet, especially if you're using the built-in mic, as these things tend to be quite sensitive to ambient noise levels.

Relative Tuning

As your ear improves, you'll be able to tune by ear, and arguably the most common method of doing this is by *relative tuning*, whereby the guitar is tuned to itself.

To begin with, you'll have to have something available to tune at least one string to, or the whole affair is going to be a shot in the dark. If you're playing with another instrument, you'll end up tuning to that most of the time, anyway, as other instruments aren't necessarily as friendly as the guitar is in terms of tuning. For instance, if you're playing with a pianist, it would be extremely unwise to suggest that he should tune to you!

In any case, you probably know already that, under normal circumstances, a guitar is tuned like this:

Bass	E
	A
	D
	G
	B
Treble	E

Relative tuning calls for each string to be tuned to another and takes advantage of the fact that the instrument is absolutely ridden with duplicate pitches (see previous chapter). For instance, if you play the bass E string at the fifth fret, you'll arrive at the pitch of the fifth string, A:

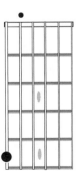

If you've somehow tuned your E string to the outside world, then obviously you'll be tuning the fifth string to the pitch of your bass E, fifth fret. This is where your ear has to be up to scratch. A good musical ear will nail the pitch to less than ten per cent of a semitone (forget the maths – that's pretty accurate) and anything too far outside these parameters is going to sound quite ugly (especially by the time you reach the top string – read on).

Once you're pretty sure that the two pitches agree, you can move onto the next pair:

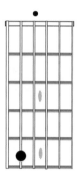

This time, you're playing a D on the A string (ie the one you've just tuned), so you've got to make any adjustments necessary to the pitch of the fourth string.

It's the same story for the fourth and third strings, too:

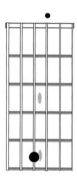

But once we reach the third and second string pair, you're matching pitches at the third string, fourth fret:

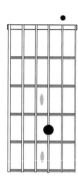

There's nothing too scientific about this sudden change; it's just the way the guitar is tuned.

Once we've reached the top pair, things have returned to normal and we're back to tuning the top string to the pitch produced at the second string's fifth fret, thus:

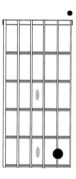

Once you've completed all of these moves, it would be nice to think that the guitar should be in tune, but unfortunately this is the real world and several things could have got in the way of tuning perfection. For a start, there's the cumulative errors of relative tuning to consider. If you were a little bit out when you tuned the sixth and fifth strings together, this error would have compounded and increased proportionately so that, by the time you reached the top pair, things would be jarringly out of tune. And so the chances are that you'll have to repeat the process a couple of times before the guitar actually starts to sound healthy again.

It's a frustrating process in the early days, and this is why I suggest you limit your frustrations accordingly by buying an electronic tuner and using the relative-tuning process only occasionally. (Ironically, this actually helps your ear by forcing you into a position where you have to match pitches.)

Tuning With Harmonics

Another (and, arguably, more scientific) way of tuning is to use harmonics. This is considered to be a tuning technique for the slightly more advanced, inasmuch as it presupposes that you can play harmonics. If you're still unsure, or just slightly bemused, I'll tell you that a harmonic is produced when you lightly stop a guitar string at the twelfth fret, for instance (you'll find harmonics everywhere), without pressing it down, and then apply just enough pressure for the string to register on your fingertip and pick the note. What should happen is that you hear a doorbell-like note. It might sound a little redundant in its basic form, but believe me, in the hands of an expert like Tommy Emmanuel, it can turn your guitar into a whole new instrument.

In any case, tuning via harmonics is usually more accurate and less hit and miss than tuning by ear – at least, in the early stages it is. Here, instead of tuning using pitches that are the same on pairs of strings, we're tuning using harmonics that agree. The difference is that you don't have to rely fully on your ear to hear the difference, because this is where science steps in and lends a hand.

If two harmonics of the same pitch are slightly out of tune, you'll hear them "beating" against each other. This means that you'll literally hear them disagreeing. (Listen to the CD for an example.) By adjusting the tuning of one of the pair, you'll end up with a single, even pitch.

To tune with harmonics, start with the bass E string and sound the harmonic at the fifth fret, then compare this to the pitch found by sounding the harmonic on the neighbouring A string's seventh fret. They should both agree exactly. If they don't, you'll hear the beating effect demonstrated on the CD. Once you've brought these two pitches into sync, move on to do the same thing on the next pair, the A and D strings. Once again, the harmonics on the fifth and seventh frets should both agree and produce a continuous tone without any beating. After this, you can effectively repeat the process for the other pairs of strings, with the exception of the G and B strings. On these two strings, the harmonics won't agree, because these two are tuned a third apart, as opposed to fourths as before. (This just means that the notes G and B are three notes away from each other along the scale, whereas A and D are four.) So, for the G and B strings, you'll have to resort to the other method of relative tuning detailed above.

Tuning with harmonics is more accurate than the previous method of relative tuning because of the exact mathematics that are involved – the beating will only stop when the two pitches are identical. Under normal circumstances, this will be more accurate than merely listening to two pitches and trying to match them up. Then, all you've got to worry about is the same compound error that we saw before – by the time you've reached the top pair of strings (if you started at the bottom), any slight errors incurred while tuning the previous pairs of strings will have combined to give you an unsatisfactory result.

Tuning Quirks

Be prepared to read about players who tune various strings sharp or flat because they're addressing the quirks of their own ears. For instance, it's not uncommon for players of electric guitars (especially those guitars with light-gauge strings) to tune the bass E string slightly flat to avoid an anomaly whereby this string actually tends to go sharp the harder you pluck it. (Try it!) So they compensate by tuning it slightly flat – not so much that it's out of tune but just enough to allow for this particular phenomenon.

The jazz player Martin Taylor actually tunes his whole guitar sharp. Whereas the tuning standard for pretty much all Western instruments (except Martin's) is A = 440Hz – which means that a vibration of 440 cycles per second produces the pitch that should be found at the fifth fret on your top E string – Martin tunes to A = 442, which is very, very close but slightly sharp. This has the effect of making the guitar stand out slightly in an ensemble, and Martin says that it makes up for the fact that he plays clean and without too much vibrato.

PAINLESS MUSIC THEORY I – CHORDS

"I have this thirst for knowledge at the moment, much more than I did when I was younger, and I just want to know these things and be able to play these things. I said to Andrew [Bown] a couple of years ago, 'I wish I'd known this when I was younger.' He said, 'Oh no!' And I said, 'What do you mean, "Oh no?"' And he said, 'Well, you wouldn't have written "Down Down" or "Caroline"; You'd have started saying, "No, I'm going to have to throw something clever in here."' Because there is the danger that the musician gets involved. It's all right us saying we want to be musicians and all that shit, but if you're not careful… 'Caroline', I'd start throwing ninths in or 13s and you go, 'What the fuck for?' So perhaps things have gone as they were supposed to. Perhaps. I just think I should have learned… But that goes for my whole life, school and education. I have quite a thing for languages – I could have spoken at least three or four languages; I like them. And I was stupid at school – it was, 'No, I'm going to be a rock 'n' roll star. You lot can fuck off.' And I was right – I *did* make it, I suppose. But they were right – I missed the knowledge. I have a thirst for knowledge at 47 years old. What a dickhead! What a time to wake up." *Francis Ross*i

It always comes as a shock to students of guitar that they have to know anything about music theory. The main complaint I get faced with as a teacher is, 'But I only want to play guitar for fun. Why do I have to learn any theory?' I try to calm things down by assuring my students that they only need to know enough theory to benefit them, that knowing it will actually help them play better, learn faster and generally be less grumpy with their instrument when they can't fathom out something.

I encourage pupils to analyse their own problems and find ways of overcoming them independently. This means that their progress is far more consistent, even when I'm not around to ask questions (although I must admit that my telephone number is ex-directory, just in case).

The other thing I tell them is that I'll keep all the theory that they have to learn at an absolute minimum. I'm going to make the same promise here, too; I don't want this book to start looking like a highly stylistic version of the *Highway Code*, after all. If theory is what you specifically need, maybe you're the type of person who needs all the questions answered ("What exactly is figured bass and why was it prevalent during the Baroque period?"). If that's the case, there are loads of books on the market – and a whole world of pain available to you over the Internet, if you've got the patience to put just the right words into a search engine that will actually help you find what you're looking for and not just another list of Japanese hi-fi manufacturers and Miami-based holiday locations. (I once tried to find an email address for the Japanese *Guitar Magazine* and so I keyed in the words "Japanese guitar magazine" into a search engine and was rewarded with a list of, ahem, adult sites. Suddenly, I envied the Amish.)

So which areas of the labyrinthine world of music theory are actually going to be of use in our pursuit of learning to play acoustic guitar? I guess that the first zone we have to explore is that of chords – you're definitely going to be playing some, and so knowing a few simple ground rules is going to be of benefit. Everyone ready?

Cooking With Chords

If it wasn't for all of the chord books on the market, there'd be a lot more forests left in the world. Don't get me wrong, I'm not against anyone owning one. In fact, I think everyone setting out to learn guitar should go and buy one. It's just that they tend to be misused, in my opinion. I tell people that they should treat them like dictionaries rather than tutors. You're not going to learn what chords you need to memorise by browsing through a chord book. The only way you'll learn that kind of information is by playing songs, literally trying to put something new in front of you and regularly trying to play through it. In this way, you'll soon see which chords are cropping up on a regular basis and

which ones you should prioritise in your learning regime. Occasionally, it may be that you'll have to look up an alternative voicing or "shape" at some other point on the neck because it seems to fit in with the song you're learning that much better. Otherwise, my advice is to leave the book on the shelf and refer to it sparingly. Actually finding out a bit about chords will fill in a lot of the blanks for you and make you a whole lot less dependent on your chord book, believe me.

So where do we begin? Well, probably the first thing we should look for is some common ground. I'm taking for granted that you'll have come across a lot of the first-position chord voicings, such as the ones shown here:

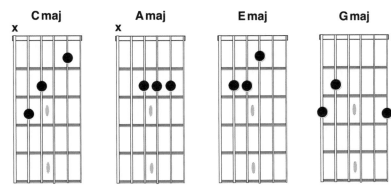

Example 1

I tend to refer to these chords as "campfire chords" because they're the ones everyone learns to play their first songs. (I imagine people sitting around campfires singing 'Michael, Row The Boat Ashore' because that's as far as they got when they were learning, y'see? Humour me.)

What we have in Example 1 is pretty much your starter's pack of chords – agreed? They are simple in operation and quite easy to use in songs, too. Well, if there was a common denominator here, it's the fact that all of these chords are *triads*. (Oops, jargon alert! Remember I promised I'd keep the music buzz-words and street-talk to an absolute minimum? I haven't forgotten, either; the word *triad* is one of those words it's advisable to know out there in the real world.) All that *triad* means is "three notes" – or, at least, as far as we're concerned it does. It means something entirely different in Chinatown, so people tell me.

Anyway, a triad is three notes of a scale played together that supports a melody over the top. Triads are usually three specific notes of a scale, in most instances the first, third and fifth. Take a look at this:

C	D	E	F	G	A	B	C
1	2	3	4	5	6	7	1

If we take the first, third and fifth notes from the C-major scale shown above, we end up with these notes – a C-major triad, in fact:

C	E	G
1	3	5

Now, if I told you that all of the six-, five- or four-note versions of the chord of C major that you might have come across in your travels contain these notes and *only* these notes, you might not want to believe me, but I can prove it. Observe:

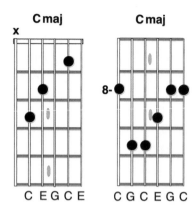

Cmaj   **Cmaj**

C E G C E   C G C E G C

You see? There might be a few repeats in there, but there are only the notes from the triad contained in the chord shape, as long as its name is C major. (I like proving things – it makes me understand how Pythagoras must have felt.)

Of course, the same trick works for other chords, too. If we take a D-major scale and apply the same logic, let's see where we end up:

D	E	F#	G	A	B	C#	D
1	2	3	4	5	6	7	1

This means that our triad from this scale would look like this:

D	F#	A
1	3	5

And guess what? If we look at a couple of familiar chord shapes for D major…

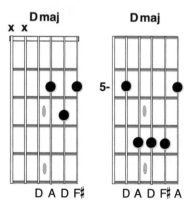

Dmaj   **Dmaj**

D A D F#   D A D F# A

Beginning to make sense? And if you're wondering if the same kind of logic applies to minor chords, fear not. I feel another example coming up…

A	B	C	D	E	F	G	A
1	2	3	4	5	6	7	1

What you see above is a scale of A minor. If we take the first, third and fifth once again, we end up with this:

A	C	E
1	3	5

And if we look at one of the familiar chord shapes for A minor…

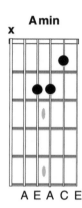

Amin

A E A C E

The magic's still there, eh? But there is one very important difference between major and minor chords, and that opens up an entirely different can of beans.

Intervals

Before we move on, it's time for another swift definition. You'll probably come across the word *interval* in your musical travels, and so it would probably be wise for me to take a couple of paragraphs to tell you exactly what these things are.

Basically, there are two different types of interval: harmonic and melodic. Stop cowering with fear! The explanation is simpler than you think.

An interval is, quite simply, the distance between notes in either a scale or melody (that's the melodic variation) or between the notes in a chord. (If you're nodding sagely to yourself, thinking, "I bet that's the harmonic type," award yourself a pat on the back.) So, if I was to say to you that a C-major triad contains the first, third and fifth intervals of the scale of C, you might see just how harmless an item we're dealing with here.

The only complication enters our lives when we start to consider the distance between the notes in the triad themselves. For instance, we know that the interval between C and E is a third, and, partly because it belongs to a major scale, we'll define it even further by calling it a *major third*, just to make sure. But what about the gap between the E and the G? This is where it's probably best to play both of these notes along a single string on your guitar and count the frets between them. Let's do this first for C and E. Take the C at the first fret on your B string and the E at the fifth fret and count the frets that separate them. You should have made it five, which is great because that's dead right. Now, if we do the same maths for E and G, we'll come up with a different figure altogether. Stick with the E at the fifth fret of the B string and find the G at the eighth fret on the same string. Count again. This time, the answer is four frets. To paraphrase Spiñal Tap's Nigel Tufnel, that's one less, innit?

So we have the sum that the interval in a major third (the gap between C and E) is five frets, or five *semitones*, to give the thing a more authentic musical identity. But E to G is only four semitones, so what's that distance called in interval-speak? Believe it or not, it's called a minor third. I can prove this, too. Look again at the A minor scale I've detailed above. The first and third notes are A and C – agreed? Now look at the distance along a guitar string once again. Take the A on the fifth fret of the top E string. The nearest C on the same string is at fret eight. Count the frets and you come up with four – a minor third.

Now, I know that this can be a real headache to come to terms with, and I remember my promise not to enslave you with jargon-encrusted text, but this is something that you will come up against. The term *interval* is used quite freely in musical circles, especially during talk about chords, and so you're going to need a sort of pocket definition, at least. Here's a list with the relevant fret values. (You don't have to commit these to memory or even worry about them unduly; they're just here as a reference.)

Minor second	C-C#	two frets
Major second	C-D	three frets
Minor third	C-E♭	four frets
Major third	C-E	five frets
Fourth	C-F	six frets
Flat fifth	C-G♭	seven frets
Fifth	C-G	eight frets
Sharp fifth	C-G#	nine frets
Sixth	C-A	ten frets
Flat seventh	C-B♭	eleven frets
Major seventh	C-B	twelve frets
Octave	C-C	13 frets

So, if you want to know what the interval was between the notes G and D, count the frets between them *inclusively* and check the chart above. You should find that there are eight frets between these two notes and that this would make it a fifth. It's as simple as that. Of course, everything goes misty again when we begin to talk about intervals like ninths, 13ths and so on. You'll be relieved that the logic remains the same, but before we meet these new members of the interval clan, it's time to press on and meet the chord families.

Chord Families

"I had an advantage in that I was studying music theory at high school while I was learning about the guitar, so I knew how to analyse chords on manuscript paper – I knew what the chords contained, in terms of notes. So I would look at my guitar neck and go, 'OK, if I want to make a D-minor 13, I know I've got to have a root, a third, a seventh, a sixth, a ninth and a fifth. I'd realise that, on guitar, that's kind of difficult, right? For practicality, you've got to eliminate some things. In fact, the whole beauty of arrangement is what to eliminate. But I'd be able to do things like that in order to hear them. I'd realise that there were many ways to play a major-seventh chord and each sounded slightly different." *Joe Satriani*

Believe it or not, there is a system to help you through all this chord-learning business. I know that a casual browse through a chord book – one with a title like

Bumper Chord Compendium For Guitar: Every Chord You'll Ever Need To Know! – can be a little daunting; it's a case of too many chords, not enough fretboard, half the time. But we can systemise things quite nicely and put a lot of this option-anxiety to rest.

For a start, it's helpful to believe that there are basically three family groups of chords: major, minor and dominant seventh. That's probably already cheered you up a bit, but it gets better. First, let's take a look at how the basic family groups can be defined.

The Majors

You can spot one of these particular family members pretty much straight away. In almost every case, the chord name will have "maj" or "major" attached to it, for a start. So you would be dealing with chords like these:

A maj   C maj   B maj

Nothing too controversial there. But the major family is a little more expansive than that. Look at this group:

A maj7   C maj6   B maj9

All of the above chords belong to the family of majors. Think of it this way: they may all sound slightly different, but the family resemblance is unmistakable in context. In order to explain this a little more fully, we're going to have to get slightly more technical for a few paragraphs. Stick with it – there's nothing too scary coming up.

A little while ago, we looked at how basic major chords are made up. Take a major scale, extract its first, third and fifth notes, play them together and you have the basic ingredients of a major chord. To enlarge on that basic formula, it's true to say that you can add any other note from the scale to that basic major triad and you'll arrive at a few variations on the major theme.

Let's take the chord of C maj7 as an example. Take another look at the scale:

C	D	E	F	G	A	B	C
1	2	3	4	5	6	7	1

We already know where the basic major chord comes from:

C	E	G
1	3	5

And the "maj7" bit comes from simply adding the seventh note of the scale to that basic framework. Think of it as a little like cooking, where you add ingredients to bring out different flavours. If you look at the scale above, you'll see that the seventh note of the C-major scale is B, so it's not going to be a huge surprise that the recipe for a C maj7 chord would be this:

C	E	G	B
1	3	5	7

In order to hear the difference between these two chords, play them yourself. Below are two examples where the difference is really pronounced:

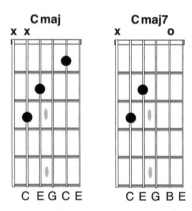

Play these chords one after the other and you'll hear what's going on. Remember that it's important to see what's going on, visually, but far more important for you to learn the difference in sound between the two. It's one thing to have a chord book on your bookshelf, but it's even better to have one inside your head.

Of course, this trick works throughout the family of major chords. Now let's take another couple of examples. Take the chord C maj6, for example. (A word or two of caution here: sometimes "major sixth" chords miss out the word *major* from their chord titles.

Don't ask me why. Put it down to the fact that there's always someone who has to be different. Remember, I don't make the rules; I only work here.)

So back to our C maj6 example. Remember the recipe? Take the basic triad and add the sixth note of the scale for flavour, as below:

```
C   E   G   A
1   3   5   6
```

Take a look (and a listen) to these chord shapes:

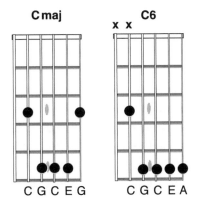

Examine the difference between them and, if you like, categorise them somehow. In my mind, a sixth chord always reminds me of the way in which The Beatles sometimes used to end their early singles. Listen to this variation on the sixth-chord-shape theme:

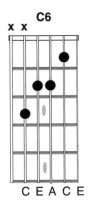

It's really useful to have some sort of sonic reference point for the different chord types like this, and on this point, at least, I'm not really in a position to make that

many suggestions. It really is better if you build up a set of reference points that are unique to you. You'll remember them better this way.

Naturally, with something as fickle as music, you'd expect there to be some more exceptions to the rule, wouldn't you? Well, hang onto your seats.

A good place to start would be major ninth chords. Just a quick look will tell you that there are only seven notes in the scale and so something must have gone horribly wrong somewhere down the line. It's another of music's quirks that the initial numbering system for notes on the scale goes slightly awry at this point, but the answer's not half as daunting as the question might make you believe.

Look at this:

```
C D  E  F  G  A  B  C  D  E  F  G  A  B  C
```

What we have here is two scales of C major laid end to end. Technically, we would say that there are two octaves of C in front of us. *Octave* just means eight notes – you count the root (C) twice, once at the bottom and once at the top. So a single scale of C would represent one octave. Add another and you've got two.

The real lunacy begins when we come to numbering this extended scale. You might like to think that it goes from one to 15, but music is great at resisting the obvious. Check this out:

```
C D  E  F  G  A  B  C  D  E  F  G  A  B  C
1 2  3  4  5  6  7  1  9  3  11 5  13 7  1
```

At first glance, this might seem a little ridiculous, but I'll try to explain it as simply as I can. It's good old music convention that gives us two octaves of a scale numbered in this way. What's happened is that we've kept the important numbers from the first octave and kept them in place for the second. So we retain one, three and five (which are triad members and very important) and, for reasons that may or may not become apparent later on, we keep the seven, too. So, if you take another look at the bizarre maths above once again, you might be able to begin to make some sense of it.

Remember when we looked at intervals a few headaches ago? I said that I'd leave the ninths and so on until later, and now I guess that moment's here. Hopefully, you can understand how a note can have two numbered positions in the scale – in the case of D, it's both a major second and a ninth. (It's actually unlikely that you'll need another chart to count the frets between these "over the octave" intervals; it's more important for you to realise that a second becomes a ninth, a fourth becomes an eleventh, a sixth turns into a 13th.) This, then, explains why we have chords with titles like "C maj9". Have a look here at the recipe for that particular chord:

$$
\begin{array}{ccccc}
C & E & G & B & D \\
1 & 3 & 5 & 7 & 9
\end{array}
$$

You'll notice straight away that the seventh has somehow managed to gatecrash the C maj9 party. This is another curiosity of formal music harmony. Major ninth chords usually have the seventh in them, too. It's just a fact of life. (We'll look at what happens if you miss it out in a minute.)

Here's a before-and-after example of a major ninth at work:

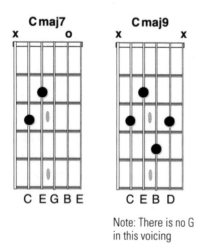

Note: There is no G in this voicing

This is a very sweet-sounding chord. It's also very dense, harmonically. We've added two notes from the scale to the original triad and everything is beginning to get harmonically saturated. This brings us neatly to what I call "Mead's First Law of Chords" – that the more notes from the scale you add to the triad, the less you can do with it. What I mean by this can be very neatly demonstrated. Go and get a guitar while I warm up my demonstrating facilities… Below, you'll find two bars of music that ask you to play the chord of C major four times to the bar:

‖ C maj / / / | C maj / / / ‖

Nothing too controversial there. The sound of the basic C-major triad is so open and simple that you could play it easily for around eight bars before it began to wear out its welcome. But try this:

‖ C maj9 / / / | C maj9 / / / ‖

It doesn't really work, does it? The overall sweetness gets a little bit too much very quickly. To me, it's the equivalent of toffees – one or two are nice, but you wouldn't want to live on them. So that's Mead's First Law of Chords in a nutshell. To sum up, you could say that the more "extended" chords are useful for splashes of colour but that nothing beats good old basic chords for everyday use.

As a revision tool, and to really hammer home this point about chord recipes, here's a list of some popular chord variations in the key of C:

Basic triad (C maj)	C	E	G			
	1	3	5			
Major sixth (C6)	C	E	G	A		
	1	3	5	6		
Major seventh (C maj7)	C	E	G	B		
	1	3	5	7		
Major ninth (C maj9)	C	E	G	B	D	
	1	3	5	7	9	
Major six nine* (C6/9)	C	E	G	A	D	
	1	3	5	6	9	
Major seventh (six nine)	C	E	G	A	B	D
(C maj7 [6/9])	1	3	5	6	7	9

You've probably guessed that, because the six-nine chord has earned itself an asterisk, it's another special case. Well, that's true, but only from the point of view that it's another chord that needn't necessarily have the word *major* attached to its title. Teaching music theory is a little like teaching chess, sometimes – it's full of odd moves and strange rules. And while we're on the subject of weirdness, here comes the suspended chord.

Suspended (Sus) Chords

"I get more satisfaction from playing a suspended chord in the middle of a verse than I do from playing an amazing solo." Dominic Miller

For convenience, I tend not to consider these as chords in the truest sense of the definition. They are more like harmonic devices that end up as chords from rather bizarre beginnings. Don't panic, they're very common and simple to use; it's just the definition that sounds a little strange. Whereas we've seen that all C-major chords contain the basic C triad, this one doesn't – at least, at first it doesn't. Let me explain. A "sus" chord is really a chord in two parts: a suspension and a resolution. A basic C sus4 would be made up like this:

$$C \quad F \quad G$$
$$1 \quad 4 \quad 5$$

And it would look like this:

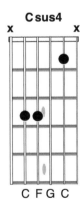

C sus4

C F G C

If you play it, you'll hear why they call it a suspended chord – it doesn't really sound like it's finished, does it? What's more, if you check out the chord recipe for it, you'll see that there's no third. All of a sudden, the

F has crept in there instead. Surely some mistake! But no, this is all perfectly normal. However, the character of the sus chord is only fully realised when it's followed by a straightforward major chord. Play this:

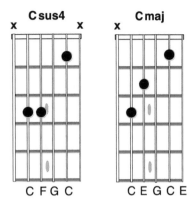

C sus4   **C maj**

C F G C   C E G C E

Sounds much better, doesn't it? See what I mean about it being more of a harmonic device in two parts rather than a stand-alone chord?

You might also run across a suspended second chord. This would look like this in its basic recipe form:

$$C \quad E \quad G \quad D$$
$$1 \quad 3 \quad 5 \quad 9 \ (2)$$

If you check back to our chart that showed two octaves of the C-major scale, you'll notice that the note D enjoys a sort of dual identity, being both the second and the ninth, in terms of its relationship to C. Usually, this chord would take advantage of the close relationship between C and D in the scale (ie the fact that they're neighbours). This gives rise to another harmonic effect very similar to that of the "sus4" we've just seen. Here's a chord diagram:

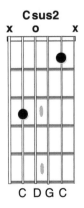

C sus2

C D G C

Sounds a little strange, doesn't it? But not nasty. Now try it again, this time resolving it into a straight major:

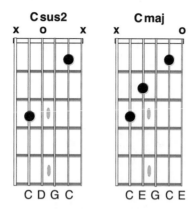

C sus2

x o x

C D G C

C maj

x x o

C E G C E

Sounds a bit better than before, wouldn't you say? This is because the major chord has given the sus2 an identity, a musical function. Without this resolution, it's a little like a hinge without a door attached to it.

There's also a chord that has a very similar recipe to the sus2 but carries a different name. This is the C add9 chord. Now, you know about the note D's dual identity in the scale of C, and we've heard what it sounds like in its role as second. This chord takes advantage of that other personality: the ninth.

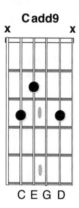

C add9

x x

C E G D

Compare the sound of a sus2 with that of an add9, I think you'll agree, there's a big difference – and yet we're dealing with the same note being added to the basic triad. This goes some way to illustrate how you can bring out very different effects just by mixing up the notes within a chord, and it's a very good example of why it's good to know several versions of a chord, not just one.

The Minor Family

"Say, for instance, you're playing in C minor… You say to yourself, 'OK, I've got a C minor seventh, arpeggio tones – C, E♭, G and B♭ – and, say, the ninth, D. Everything else I play will merely be a connecting point." John Etheridge

Once you've read and understood the basic make-up of the family of majors, the minor family tree isn't going to provide too many shocks. Just as most families are awash with aunts, uncles, cousins and so on, families of musical chords have the same sorts of relationships cropping up time and again. As an example, here's a C-minor scale with the familiar numbering system printed underneath.

C D E♭ F G A B C
1 2 3 4 5 6 7 1

Here's another:

Ascending: C D E♭ F G A E C
1 2 3 4 5 6 7 1

Descending: C D E♭ F G A♭ E♭ C
1 2 3 4 5 6 7 1

Why two? Well, you'll notice straight away how a couple of flat signs (♭) have crept into the proceedings, and this is probably a good time to point out the differences between major and minor scales in general. It's important, because this is as vital in music as gender differences are in life, and you know how important it is to be able to tell those apart…

For a start, the harmony of the minor scale isn't half as mundane as that of the major scale. Whereas there is one basic major scale in common use, minor harmony insists on there being two, called the *melodic* and *harmonic* minor scales. Above, I've shown the harmonic followed by the melodic form. The latter of these varies depending on whether you're playing an ascending or descending version (it's true, I swear I'm not making this up) and it's the *descending* version that gives us a few of the minor-chord forms.

Because this book isn't a textbook on harmony, and because I made a promise that I was going to keep things as simple as possible and avoid weighing you down unnecessarily with the bulk of music's nuttier conventions, I'm going to talk about common usage here. After all, we only want to play some acoustic guitar and not study a degree course in music. Let's just say that minor chords are made up of elements of both melodic and harmonic minor scales. But, to begin with, let's start at a fairly basic level.

The difference between major and minor chords is better heard than explained. Here are the two triads:

Major: C E G   Minor: C E♭ G
     1 3 5   1 3 5

They're actually very similar in make-up, but if you listen to them…

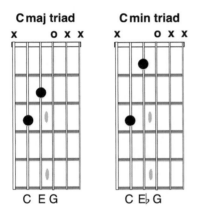

C maj triad   **C min triad**

C E G   C E♭ G

…you should be able to hear a marked difference. (If not, there's some more ear training to be done!) You can see what's happened physically on the guitar fretboard, too – you've moved one finger back a fret to play the minor. So what's going on musically at this point? Well, pretty much the same – E flat is a semitone below E, just as your finger traced out on the fretboard a moment ago. (Of course, for all I know, you're reading this on a train and have skipped the practical examples. In this case, tie a knot in something and try later.) Realistically, that's all you need to know, but if curiosity really is one of your strong points, check out any of the music-theory books available. They'll fill in all the blanks.

So all of the basic minor chords are made up from the basic minor triad. It's only when we start adding notes to the triad that we need to grab notes from the two different scales shown above.

Let's look at the sixth first, just as we did with the major chords. The recipe is very similar:

C E♭ G A
1   3   5 6

(You'll notice that this chord contains A and not A♭). Now play the following example and listen to the result:

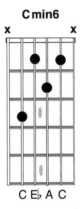

C min6

C E♭ A C

Note: This voicing omits the G

How about a minor seventh? The recipe for this contains the B♭:

C E♭ G B♭
1   3   5 7

And here's a chord voicing:

C min7

C G B♭ E♭ G

I bet you're curious why we don't use the B from the harmonic minor in this chord. Well, let's try it. Here's the recipe, followed by the chord itself:

C E♭ G B
1   3   5   7

C min (maj7)
x   o   x

C E♭ G B

That's why! It's not a very pleasant-sounding chord, is it? And yet it has its uses (The Beatles use it in 'Michelle' and it's in the second chord of Led Zeppelin's 'Stairway To Heaven', for instance). Remember, we're talking common usage here, and you'll probably agree that the B♭ sounds better in this context.

To take another example, let's consider the minor-ninth chord. (Don't forget where the nine comes from – it's just two minor scales laid end to end. As with the major-chord family, we keep the root, third, fifth and seventh notes but then find new numbers such as ninths, elevenths and 13ths creeping into that second octave.)

The basic recipe for a minor ninth looks like this:

C E♭ G B♭ D
1   3   5   7   9

Note how we're sticking with the B♭ for this chord, too. And now here's a chord shape to listen to:

C min9
x   x

C E♭ B♭ D

Note: This voicing omits the G

Incidentally, you might be wondering if there is such a thing as a minor suspended equivalent. Well, the answer to this is yes and no. If you think about it, a suspended chord doesn't contain a third, and it's the third that determines the gender of a chord – whether it's major or minor. If this isn't there in the first place, there can't be any such thing as a minor suspended chord. However, a sus chord can resolve to a minor chord in exactly the same way as it does to a major:

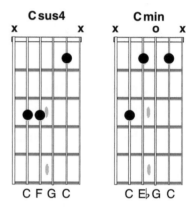

C sus4
x   x

C F G C

C min
x   o   x

C E♭ G C

It's the chord resolution that sounds different. The actual "sus" chord doesn't effectively change.

So, to sum up the minor-chord family, the most common types of chord you're going to come across are probably these, once again listed in C minor:

Basic triad (C min):	C	E♭	G		
	1	3	5		
Minor sixth (C min6):	C	E♭	G	A	
	1	3	5	6	
Minor seventh (C min7):	C	E♭	G	B♭	
	1	3	5	7	
Minor ninth (C min9):	C	E♭	G	B♭	D
	1	3	5	7	9
Minor six nine (C min6/9):	C	E♭	G	A	D
	1	3	5	6	9
Minor (major) seventh:	C	E♭	G	B	
(C min [maj] 7)	1	3	5	7	

The last one is that 'Michelle' chord once again.

If you're unfamiliar with any of the above shapes, by all means look them up in a chord book so you can hear what they sound like. But remember, it's just like looking up a word in a dictionary – you won't be able to hear the chord properly until it's been placed in context. A chord of C min (maj7) sounds ghastly when played by itself but sounds fine in the context of the songs mentioned above.

The Dominant Family

One of the most instant and striking differences between this family and the other two that we've looked at is that, with a dominant chord, we don't actually start with a basic triad. The reasons for this are all intertwined in the guts of music theory and not really worth going into here. Once again, if I've aroused your curiosity, feel free to read up on the dominant chord and its derivations in the theory book of your choice, but at present you don't need to know, just as you can quite happily drive along a motorway without knowing the recipe for asphalt.

So what do we actually start out with? In actual fact, it's a major triad with the addition of another scale member. Take a look at a dominant scale:

C D E F G A B♭ C
1 2 3 4 5 6 7 1

You'll immediately notice (I hope) that this scale bears an uncanny resemblance to the C-major scale, except for one note: B♭. This one altered note makes the scale sound almost totally different, as indeed the chords derived from it are different. To make this absolutely clear, play these two chords, a C major and a C7:

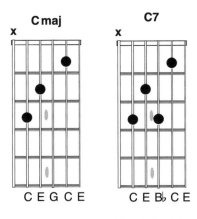

C maj   **C7**

C E G C E   C E B♭ C E

Note: This voicing omits the G

Where the ordinary C-major chord sounds final and rested, the C7 somehow sounds restless and unfinished. If you don't agree, try playing C major for a couple of bars and then put a C7 at the end. Musically speaking, you should be able to hear a "comma" as opposed to a "full stop". The C7 sounds like it desperately wants to go somewhere else, whereas the C major sounds like it's quite content to stay exactly where it is.

This is an important factor to note about dominant chords. Their function in music is more or less to be signposts, pointing the listener in a new direction, whether this be "home" to a major chord or onwards somewhere else. Like we saw with suspended chords, they demand some sort of resolution or the music won't be happy.

Try this experiment:

|| Cmaj / / / | C7 / / / | Fmaj / / / ||

If that were a sentence, it would sound properly punctuated and grammatically correct, much more so than this:

|| Cmaj / / / | Cmaj / / / | C7 / / / ||

The fact is that the C7 chord was absolutely begging to go somewhere else and the F major chord provided it a safe haven. Maybe now you can see a bit more clearly what I mean about dominant chords playing the role of musical signposts.

But let's strip a dominant chord down to its basic component parts and take a look at what makes it tick. Here's what a naked C7 looks like:

C E G B♭
1 3 5 7

Four notes instead of three this time and a nice succinct chord title – a simple "C7" would identify this little critter. Now let's take a look at two octaves of a dominant scale, just as we did when we looked at the major scale:

C D E F G A B♭ C D E F G A B♭ C
1 2 3 4 5 6 7 1 9 3 11 5 13 7 1

You don't find dominant chords with a number less than seven after the letter name. Let's look at a few examples:

C7: C E G B♭
    1 3 5 7

C9: C E G B♭ D
    1 3 5 7 9

C11: C E G B♭ D F
     1 3 5 7 9 11

C13: C E G B♭ D F A
     1 3 5 7 9 11 13

You might have noticed here that ninth chords keep the seventh, that eleventh chords keep the seventh and the ninth, and so on. This is another of music's little quirks and is nothing particularly deep and technical.

You might also have noticed one very important physiological fundamental. If you've just said to yourself, "I'm running out of fingers!", you'd be absolutely right. There's pretty much no way you can be expected to play seven notes on a six-stringed instrument, and yet the laws of music seem to be demanding this. It's all right for pianists, with no fewer than ten fingers and loads of notes to spare, but we poor guitarists with six strings and four fingers seem to be in for a difficult time if we're expected to stretch our natural resources to include of all this musical information. So what's going on?

We've run headlong into another of music's little quirks and one that is particularly relevant to the guitar. It also appears to contradict what I said a couple of paragraphs ago, but like I say, don't blame me, etc.

The answer to the dearth-of-fingers conundrum is actually quite a simple one. If you haven't got enough fingers to play a textbook-perfect version of a chord, don't. Miss out a couple of notes if you have to. It's not going to matter much in the overall scheme of things.

Now, this may appear a little like musical heresy, but before anyone starts building bonfires and burning effigies in my image, let me explain. Missing notes out of chords in music is probably more common than you might think. Obviously, a heavyweight chord like a 13th, positively bristling with its seven notes, can tend to be a bit cumbersome, even for pianists and orchestras, so composers have to find clever ways of suggesting the essence of chords without having to go the whole nine yards, as it were. If you like, I'll introduce you to Mead's Second Law of Chords (and it's also a law that covers a great deal of music in general):

"If Bach did it, it's OK."

This law can actually get you quite a long way in music theory, although examiners won't necessarily be on your side. Theory books are full of sentences like, "Never, ever, ever do this…" and then go on to give examples of how Mozart, Bach, Berlioz, Stravinsky and co did exactly what they're preaching at you not to do.

"I once read this book on counterpoint and on the very first page it said, 'You may not write the following intervals.' The intervals were F and A – a major third – expanding to E and B, a fifth. It also said you could not write G and B – a major third – expanding to F and C, a fifth. So I played these things on the piano and said, 'Why? Why can't we do this? This sounds great!' I figured that, if on the first page they were telling me that I would have to be going against something my ear immediately liked, then why should I learn the rest of that stuff?" *Frank Zappa*

When you think about it, we're talking about the apparent misbehaviour of some of the saints of classical music and not some of contemporary music's acknowledged "bad boys" – you know, the ones who play that nasty rock music.

So how do we go about suggesting the essence of certain chords without actually playing them? If you think about it, the basic difference between major and minor chords can be summed up here:

C + E = major sounding / C + E♭ = minor sounding

Agreed? If in doubt, play these two examples:

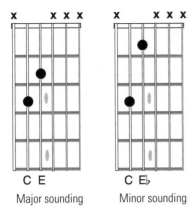

C E
Major sounding

C E♭
Minor sounding

And so, if we can convey this all-important, gender-defining characteristic in just two notes, we can play around a lot more with similar results. In fact, a dominant chord can be effectively abbreviated to this:

C + E + B♭ = dominant sounding

Here's an example of our foreshortened dominant:

C7

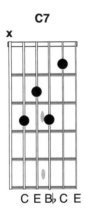

C E B♭ C E

It sounds OK, doesn't it? And yet we've missed out the fifth. Under certain circumstances, even the example below will sum up the dominant sound:

C   B♭

If you want a quick definition, what you just played is this:

C + B♭ = dominant sounding

If it still isn't clear, play the major, minor and dominant examples one after another. There is a very distinct difference.

Two other things that you have on your side when trimming down chord voicings are context and bass players. Let me explain…

Context

"Writing music and putting together songs on the guitar has led me to chord voicings and various kinds of music that I wouldn't maybe do otherwise." *John Scofield*

When you're playing a song, you are subliminally introducing your audience to a set of musical reference points and data that they probably won't even know is there. They'll take on board things like key, rhythm, melodic information, harmonic information and so on at face value without even noticing it. You can therefore afford to abbreviate some of the information, even to the point of occasionally missing things out, and the context will support everything nicely. Nothing will seem to be missing. For instance, if you've already introduced them to a certain key, they might notice a bit if you stray from it too suddenly, but they won't notice if some of the information is missed out. What's more, if you handed out a questionnaire for them to fill in, I guarantee that they wouldn't have spotted what was missing from where.

Bass Players

"I went back to thinking like a bass player on guitar and developed the bass lines before I put the top lines together. Most guitarists ask how you put bass lines onto fingerstyle pieces, and of course it's very difficult, but if you start off with a solid bass line and then add other guitar parts, in the same way that you would have a lead guitar and a rhythm guitar on the strings in between, it would all come together – if you were nifty enough." *King Rollo*

If you intend to play unaccompanied for all of your guitar-playing existence, you can skip this paragraph and put the kettle on or something. The rest of you, gather around.

An extension of what I've been saying about context can be found if you intend to play with almost any musician but with a bass player in particular. By pure job definition, a bass player tends to play a lot of chordal root notes (the "one" in the scale) and possibly no other note is capable of saying out loud, "This is the key we're playing in and here's a nice fat root to back things up." Therefore, if we're forced to be economical with chord voicings, it means that we can even afford to miss out the root note occasionally. This means that a dominant-seventh chord could look even as meagre as this:

$$E + B\flat = C7$$

This less-is-sometimes-more factor in chords is even more pronounced when both context and bass are brought into play. Take a look at this bluesy chord sequence:

|| C7 / / / | C7 / / / | F7 / / / | F7 / / / |
| C7 / / / | C7 / / / | G7 / F7 / | C7 / / / ||

Now compare what happens when you play through the sequence using first these chord voicings:

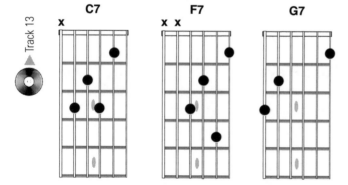

Now these:

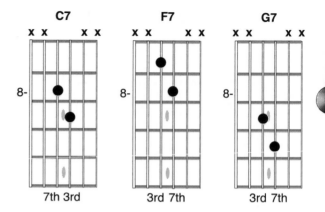

I'm hoping you thought that the first sounded fine and dandy – normal, even – but that the second, two-note variety still conveyed everything you need to know about the chord changes. Add a bass player pumping out Cs, Fs and Gs in all the right places and you've got yourself a good all-round abbreviated chord sequence.

Obviously, the two-note blues illustrated above is a pretty extreme example. We don't have to be half as Draconian under normal circumstances, but I believe that this is a good way of seeing something that's cut down to its absolute basics yet still works well.

To exhaust totally the subject of pruning chords, I'll add that it's comparatively uncommon for a classical guitar player to play full six-string chords. Most pieces in the classical repertoire simply don't call for it. Composers and arrangers prefer instead to use edited chord forms to state the harmony. And I'd invite you to take a listen to a few classical pieces. None of them sound empty of harmony, exactly, do they?

Back To The Dominant Family

So we've taken a long look at why some of the more huge chord forms sometimes miss out notes and how it's perfectly OK to do it (Bach did it, remember!). This will explain why, when you look up a chord in a chord book, sometimes a chord that the theory books demand should be brimful of notes contains only four. It's been pruned, that's all.

Extended Dominants

"I play traditional chords. There's nothing really different, although I guess the way I use them is my own. I like altered chords: flat fives, raised ninth chords, 13ths and so on. They can add a lot of character to a blues." *Robben Ford*

We've already seen how you can add notes from the dominant scale to the basic chord form and come up with a few variations along the way, but so far all we've been talking about is adding notes from within the scale, and I'm afraid it can get a bit more complicated than that, especially where dominants are concerned.

The subject of *extended dominants* might be considered more commonplace in jazz circles, but it's definitely worth a mention here. Once all of the scale tones are used up, we can dip into the non-scale tones and bag some more chord voicings, many of which are so highly "flavoured" that Mead's First Law must be invoked and they must be used with much caution.

Let's look at a chromatic scale:

C C#/Db D D#/Eb E F F#/Gb G G#/Ab A A#/Bb B C
1   b9   2   #9   3 4 #4/b5 5   #5   6   b7   7 1

Now, don't panic! Another of music's little aberrations is that sometimes we call one thing two names. (After all, if understanding this stuff was easy, they'd all be doing it, right?) So we have notes like C# and Db, which are exactly the same pitch but have a dual identity. Once again, I'm not going to go into why we do this, because the answer is crazy, but if you're insatiably curious, etc, etc…

The tones in the chromatic scale are given names that denote which notes they fall in between – for instance a "flat ninth" could only really be one note (that's one fret) flatter than the ninth, couldn't it? While a "sharp fifth" seems to spell out the fact that it might fall just one note (fret) above the fifth, agreed?

This gives us access to a whole new range of chord voicings. Here, take a look:

C7b5: C E Gb Bb
      1 3 b5 7

C7#5: C E G# Bb
      1 3 #5 7

C7b9: C E G Bb Db
      1 3 5 7   b9

C7#9: C E G Bb D#
      1 3 5 7   #9

We can even mix and match:

C7b9#5: C E G# Bb Db
        1 3 #5 7   b9

But I suspect that sensory overload is only just around the corner, so we'll leave the subject here. I might write a jazz tutor one day. Bet you can't wait!

Summary Of Chord Families
- Just about all chords fall into one of three categories: major, minor or dominant.

- All three family groups are very different in sound from each other and also different in the way they're used.

- In general, you shouldn't swap them around – for instance, don't play a minor seventh instead of a dominant or major seventh; they're different families and it just won't sound right.

- Beware that there are exceptions to the previous rule! (Now, come on, you saw that one coming, surely?) Luckily, you have to study jazz to find out why the families can be mixed up, and I'm sure you wouldn't want to go quite that far.

Some Good News
We can actually take advantage of the "family resemblance" within the three groups in a number of ways. I'll let you in on one of the more useful ways to exploit the family…

It's completely understandable that you won't be able to memorise that many chords, at least to begin with, but here's a way in which you can actually play the "wrong" chord without making a mistake.

Given that, say, C major9 and C major7 are from the same family, they are virtually interchangeable in 90 per cent of all cases. Take a look at the two chords below:

C maj9: C E G B D

C maj7: C E G B

These two chords differ from one another by only a single note, and so one chord can quite happily be substituted for the other without it sounding wrong. Therefore, if you know what a major-seventh chord shape looks like but would have to stop and think about a major ninth, by all means use the major seventh. I bet no one notices. Furthermore, if your knowledge of chords is still at the work-in-progress stage, you could substitute both of these chords for a simple major:

C maj9: C E G B D

C maj7: C E G B

C major: C E G

Can you see why? The music you're playing might have wanted you to include the note B or even B and D in the chord, but by leaving them out you've played something so similar that it definitely couldn't be termed a mistake. (Incidentally, if you ever get a gig at the local musicologists' convention and they *do* notice, forget where you heard all this, OK?)

Naturally, this substitution trick works with all of the chord families. In the minor group, feel free to use a minor seventh instead of a minor ninth, while in dire circumstances a straightforward minor of the same name will do nicely.

In the dominant family, sevenths can be used instead of ninths, 13ths and even very extended chords as long as they are fundamentally the same chords – obviously, substituting a D7 for G13♭9 isn't going to be pretty!

Distant Relationships

If you thought extended dominants were a little strange, we're about to meet some of the family that they usually keep out of sight from the public.

You may be asking yourself why I seem to have missed out the other types of chords that you might have come across: diminished and augmented. Both of these chords have a kind of nasty basic sound in that they both have a fair helping of dissonance hiding away inside them. Let's take them both one at a time.

The Diminished Chord

With the other chords we've been looking at in this chapter, we considered their arpeggios as being very much the starting point of further exploration, and I'm not going to make an exception here. A C-diminished triad looks like this:

C E♭ G♭/F♯
1 3 5

You can see right away that this looks similar to a minor triad but that something untoward has happened to the fifth: it's been flattened by a distance of one fret. If you play one of these kinds of chords, you'll hear that they're not the prettiest ones on the block, either:

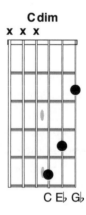

C dim
x x x

C E♭ G♭

Despite its apparent similarity, the diminished chord doesn't actually come from the minor scale; instead, it comes from the diminished scale...

C D E♭ F F♯ G♯ A B C
1 2 3 4 5 6 7 8 1

...which looks a bit of a mess, doesn't it? I mean,

how come it's got eight notes and two Fs, a natural and a sharp? The answer is that this scale doesn't really exist in the nature of music; it's one of a group of symmetrical scales that are basically man-made (hence the ugliness). However, the basic triad is natural to the world of music, very useful and, in its place, quite beautiful.

The symmetry that man has imposed on this particular scale is literally in the gaps between the notes. As far as a guitar fretboard is concerned, the "gapping" is two frets (ie one tone) followed by one fret (ie a semitone). Look at the following example, where "T" is a tone (two frets) and "st" is a semitone (one fret):

$$\overset{T}{C} - D \overset{st}{-} E\flat \overset{T}{-} F \overset{st}{-} F\sharp \overset{T}{-} G\sharp \overset{st}{-} A \overset{T}{-} B \overset{st}{}$$

Hopefully, you'll be able to see the pattern emerging. If you play the scale on the guitar, you'll hear how unpretty the whole thing sounds:

The Diminished Scale

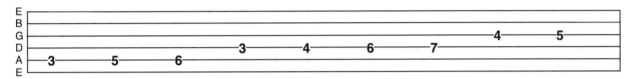

The diminished scale has its uses, but without wandering into the jazz-fusion zone it would be difficult to give any examples here, so it's probably best that you don't let this particular scale bother you too much. The diminished chord is a different matter, but we have to look at one more slight transformation first.

In its more guitar-orientated form, the diminished chord is more likely to be a diminished seventh. Take another look at the scale:

C D E♭ F F♯ G♯ A B C
1 2 3 4 5 6 7 8 1

The formula for a diminished-seventh chord looks fairly normal...

C E♭ F♯ A
1 3 5 7

...but look what's happened – because we have an eight-note scale, some of the notes aren't perhaps what you were expecting. The A is all of a sudden the seventh note, whereas we've been used to it being some kind of sixth in the past (check back, it's true). There is a (quite lengthy) explanation available to illustrate why this is so, but I'll abbreviate it here to ensure that you keep both hands on your sanity. As far as a diminished-seventh chord is concerned, the sixth note of the regular scale is looked at as a "diminished" dominant seventh (ie dropped a semitone or one fret), hence its position in the chord. If this leaves you tearing out your hair in a quandary, take my advice: just leave it and walk away. Take the diminished chord purely at face value and leave the explanation aside to ponder during unexpected long periods of solitary confinement or if you ever find yourself marooned on a desert island.

And if you thought the diminished chord was an accident waiting to happen, wait until you meet the augmented chord.

The Augmented Chord

In the same way that the diminished chord bears a resemblance to the minor scale, the augmented variety looks like it might have a cousin or two in the major household. Here's the triad:

C E G♯
1 3 5

Now take a listen to what this one sounds like:

C aug

C E G# C

so I'll show you both. But I'd like to add here that you needn't worry about this man-made-scale business too much; worry more about how the chord sounds to you and whether you think you'll be able to use it in your music. First, the whole-tone scale:

C D E F# G# A# C
1 2 3 4   5   6   7

Once again, it's not that pretty, despite the fact that it's two-thirds of a major chord. It's that sharpened fifth that adds a dollop of dissonance.

The augmented triad actually resides quite naturally in two scales, both man-made and both symmetrical,

Just as the diminished scale has more than the statutory eight notes per octave, the augmented scale has one less. (You see what happens when man messes with nature?) It's called the whole-tone scale because there is – guess what? – a whole tone between each of the notes. To you and me, this means that there's a fret's distance between each of its notes, like this:

The Whole-Tone Scale

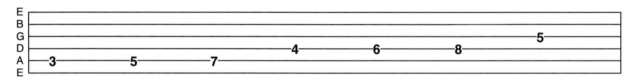

To my mind, this is where maths enters music, and I don't believe that these two disciplines really belong together. You should always play from the heart. Don't use a slide rule.

The second of the augmented triad's home neighbourhoods is called the augmented scale, and this little beast really is a weird one. It's arranged like this:

C D# E G G# B C
1 2   3 4 5   6 7

We've come up one note short again, but you can see the triad happily residing within the scale. Incidentally, this scale comprises intervals of a minor third and a semitone one after the other – more maths in music. Take a listen:

The Augmented Scale

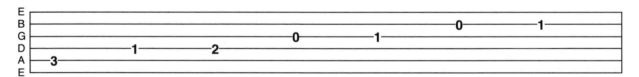

It's not pretty, is it? But never mind, it's the chord that we're really interested in.

Arguably the most common form of augmented chord around is the "7#5" variety. This chord really belongs to the altered-dominant family, as its constituent parts look like this:

C E G♯ B♭
1 3 5   7

As you can see, the note B♭ isn't the seventh of either of the scales illustrated on the previous page, which really makes this chord only an adoptive son of the augmented family group. Its nature is very similar – play the augmented and the 7♯5 chords one after another and you'll hear how close they are.

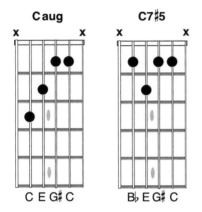

C aug **C7♯5**

C E G♯ C   B♭ E G♯ C

Note: This voicing doesn't have the root in the bass

Now that you know a bit more about both the augmented and diminished chords, put this knowledge aside and focus on the actual sounds that they produce. Find a way to catalogue them in your mind so you can remember how they sound. I tend to think of the diminished as a sort of haunted-house chord and the augmented as a sort of rock 'n' roll ballad intro – for instance, it's augmented chords that you hear at the beginning of The Beatles' 'Oh, Darling' and Chuck Berry's 'No Particular Place To Go'.

One Final Quirk

After the long slog of trying to understand exactly how these two troublemakers of the chord world sprang to life, it will come as a relief to know that learning the chord shapes is really quite easy. Because both of them are symmetrical chords, we run into symmetrical chord voicings, too. Take a look at the notes in C dim7:

C E♭ G♭ A
1 3   5   7

Now look at the notes in the chord of E♭ dim7:

E♭ G♭ A C
1   3   5 7

Look familiar? If the message isn't yet strikingly clear, take a look at the chord of G♭ dim7:

G♭ A C E♭
1   3 5 7

It's the same notes all the time. Music law states that every note in a diminished chord can be its root, which translates down to the fact that learning diminished-seventh chord shapes is a breeze, because there are only three of them. You can prove it to yourself by sitting down with a chord book and a guitar – you'll soon find that you can play only three variations of a diminished-seventh chord before all of the notes start repeating. Sometimes, learning music gives something back.

If you thought that was good news, you'll be delighted to hear that you can apply the same trick to augmented triads – not the 7♯5 variety, just the triad. Look at a C augmented chord:

C E G♯
1 3 5

Now look at one in E:

E G♯ C
1 3   5

Because there are three notes in the basic augmented triad and twelve notes in the chromatic scale, threes into twelve go four times, *ergo* there are four augmented variations. This just proves that maths can be fun, although it's rarely pretty.

Chords In General

Any token glance through a chord book will tell you that there are hundreds of variations of chords available to us as guitarists, although all of them fall into one of the chord families listed above. Most day-to-day chords will be straightforward majors, minors or dominants with a smattering of extensions. We really only dip into the dissonant areas of chord life when we look into music forms that call on them, such as jazz, for instance. You'll mostly be concerned with different voicings of quite regular chords, however, and this is where a lot of difference can be made. I'm not going to launch into a treatise on how to arrange music, but I will offer a few general rules and guidelines.

You might have heard of the term *chord inversions* and wondered how it would affect your life. Quite simply, it means… Well, here's the C-major triad once again:

C   E   G
1   3   5

Any C-major chord in any chord book you can find me will report back that these three notes form a C-major chord. But look at this…

E   G   C
3   5   1

…and this:

G   C   E
5   1   3

All that's happened here is that we've taken the triad and put the notes in a different order, but it's still C major. The thing that really makes the difference here is how different they sound to one another. Try playing them.

With each example, you can tell it's a C major chord (especially if you've got a C bass note under what you're doing), but the texture, flavour or whatever you want to call it has changed slightly. To me, the version with E on the bottom sounds more majestic, whereas the chord with G on the bottom sounds slightly less defined. But the point here is that you can apply this kind of thinking to every chord from every family group, twist them all around a bit and come up with different shades of the same chords. This is something guitar players do quite naturally, owing to the tuning of the guitar, and provides a good explanation why C major played as a barre chord at the eighth fret sounds different in nature (not just pitch) from C major played in open position down at the nut.

As you can imagine, if you apply this mix-and-match philosophy to every chord type available, you'd pretty soon be able to fill your own chord book. I haven't done the maths, but I know enough to say that you could run into many hundreds of different voicings before you exhausted your investigations.

However, I still maintain that the best way to learn chords is to learn songs. The very nature of the way in which songs are written, the various ebbs and flows of harmony itself, would dictate that you learn all of the common chord voicings first. The rest will be waiting in the wings for that time when your taste in music ventures towards the exotic.

"I realised that, even if I didn't always remember the name of something, I'd remember the sound. It's like learning a language, where you don't know the long words but after a while you recognise them, like a child. So now I say, 'That's a 13th with a flattened ninth,' because I recognise the sound." *Mark Knopfler*

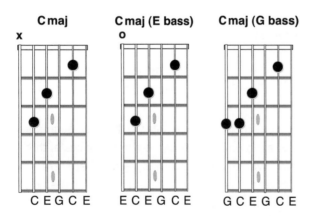

Cmaj   Cmaj (E bass)   Cmaj (G bass)

C E G C E   E C E G C E   G C E G C E

PAINLESS MUSIC THEORY II – SCALES

"I can remember my dad sitting me down and showing me some scales on the guitar and I got them under my fingers. What that did more than anything was to start to unravel the mystery of the fingerboard, in terms of where the notes were in relation to each other. But in terms of getting dexterity together, I just used to play, and I've always been like that – I would sooner use the time I have practising something I'm going to use rather than doing gymnastics or exercises. So now I never play scales or anything like that." *Martin Taylor*

Scales are, without doubt, the dullest things on Earth. They're not much fun to play; they are fairly meaningless in their basic form, musically; and they take up an awful lot of time that could be spent actually playing. The trouble is, they do you an awful lot of good.

Of course, I can say all of this with a smug smile on my face, having spent three hours a day for ages just practising the darned things when I was learning to play. But I was shooting for a music profession, remember, so don't be afraid that I'm going to suggest you should follow my example in this respect.

If you recall the deal I made with you that I wasn't going to make you do anything that wasn't really necessary, you can rest assured that this applies to scales as well. I'm not going to take you anywhere that you won't benefit from being taken. In fact, I'm going to try to make sure that what I do ask you to do is of maximum benefit to you.

If you don't mind, I'd like to tell you my thoughts on scales before we begin any serious work on the subject. Hopefully, I'll be able to lay waste to a few myths surrounding scales at the same time.

Scales – The Whole Truth

"People ask me what scales I use, but I have to tell them that it's been so long since I studied scales that I'm not sure which ones I'm actually using. A lot of times, it's not a scale – it's not just seven notes over and over again; it's tonalities with chromatic passing tones and all kinds of stuff." *John Scofield*

First of all, let's get one thing completely straight: scales are *not* music. At best, all they are is a resource with which music is built. They represent (to an extent) raw materials and not the finished product. Practising scales will do you a lot of good in the two main areas that learning an instrument demands from a student: those of aiding the physical development necessary to play and providing a lot of basic ear training at the same time.

Obviously, physical development on the instrument is necessary for a number of reasons. For one, you're asking your left and right hands to perform tasks that require muscular development and co-ordinative skills at the same time, neither of which were included in the original blueprints of human beings. Also, I don't talk about physical demands lightly – a spectator's-eye view of guitar playing might conclude that it can't actually be that difficult, but you could draw the same conclusions about ballet if you didn't read anything to the contrary. Remember the adage "If it looks like you're working, you ain't working hard enough" and you may stop to think next time you see someone play with no apparent effort at all. You can bet that, in this case, certain physical development has been addressed and decanted into every performance.

You may think that I'm actually preparing you to join the army and expecting you to commit yourself to a rigorous daily workout at the guitar boot camp for years before I consider you fit enough to drop behind audience lines. I don't, but some hard work *is* going to be necessary.

On the musical development side of things, consider this: a musician is only as good as his ear. If you're careful about what you practise, you can actually be feeding vital information into your ear at the same time. This will go a long way towards developing your own musical sensibility – your inner musical self, if you want to get all new-age about it.

An imbalance between these two practice targets can be illustrated quite simply. Someone with a good musical ear who hasn't developed his physical chops on his instrument will be in the position where he can't actually execute the music he hears in his head. He might be hearing the most world-redefining music but is powerless to play any of it. On the other side of the coin, if a guitarist develops his physical acumen to a very high degree but essentially has still got cloth ears, he won't have anything to play – or, at best, everything he does play will have to have come from something he's practised as an exercise. This results in cold, unemotional playing – and no gigs.

I'll leave you to decide which is the more commonplace deficit, but put it this way: if someone touches you emotionally with their music, you can forgive certain shortcomings in technique. If it's possible for the great instrumentalists to say more with one note than most of us can play in a weekend, how come? We can all play one note on our instruments, can't we? Nothing too technically demanding about that, surely?

"The guitar is so difficult to get your own sound on, and if I've come up with my own sound, I think it's been by luck. It's just sort of been shaped over a long period of time." *John Scofield*

I think that, for many people, a lot of time is wasted in the practice room. During the '80s and, to some extent, the '90s, too much emphasis was placed on the gymnastic side of playing an instrument and not enough on actually producing anything that was in any way emotionally valid. Music is meant to touch the soul, not the gym wall.

If it sounds like I'm preaching a bit here, I am and I'm not afraid to say so. It's something about which I believe quite passionately and I want to get the message well and truly home. We'll return to the jokes in a moment or two, fear not.

Back To The Plot

So how many scales am I asking you to go out and learn? Well, seeing as it's acoustic guitar we're talking about here, and I'm guessing you're not really interested in blistering, distortion-enriched, ten-minute-long guitar solos, then the answer's, "Oh, about four."

For those of you who are interested or possessed of a split personality where maybe your darker side actually wants to be able to whip out the odd blistering ten-minute-long solo, the answer's still, "Oh, about four."

I'll modify that last statement very slightly, if you can indulge me a moment longer. Four scales is a very good place to start, because a whole world of music is open to you with only this modest resource at your disposal. The reason for this is that most music is drawn from very simple building blocks. As we saw in the chapter on chords, if you want to venture into more arcane areas later on – jazz, for instance – you'll need to learn more or, at the very least, view the ones you're going to learn here slightly differently.

Making A Start

If you think about it, the first scale you learn ought to be the one that forms the answer to the question, "What's the most common scale in music?" The answer to this particular question is, without doubt, the major scale, which we looked at while investigating the origins of the major chord. You'll agree (I hope) that an awful lot of chords in songs tend to be major, and if you've ever been curious about key signatures (the arrangement of sharp [♯] or flat [♭] signs at the beginnings of pieces of written music) then you'll have seen that the majority of them tend to be major.

In fact, a character by the unforgettable name of Cecil Sharp (with a name like C Sharp, he wasn't going to be a mechanic, now, was he?) once conducted an exhaustive survey of Olde English folk songs and found that a startlingly high percentage (we're talking something like 95 per cent) were all in a major key.

I've probably clued you in by now to the fact that it's the major scale that we'll be looking at first.

The Major Scale

This is the scale from whence all of the great songs come. Well, OK, most of them do, at least. It's strange to think that everything from nursery rhymes to some of the great melodies of Bach, Beethoven, The Beatles and beyond are hidden within these notes. So don't look at it as being just another boring exercise; it's the parent to some extremely impressive music, and you'll only hurt its feelings if you treat it otherwise.

C Major

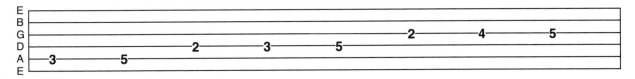

This first version of the major scale is really just for you to acclimatise yourself with the way it sounds. Play it and listen to it. Pretty soon, I'm going to ask you to sing it while you play it, so be warned.

Once again, as with the chapter on chords, I'm giving examples here in the key of C major and leaving you to expand your repertoire of keys accordingly. (The guitar is such a simple instrument to shovel information like this around on that this really isn't the daunting task that it might sound, initially.)

The Major Pentatonic Scale

This scale is a sort of abbreviated form of the major scale. If we compare the two, you'll see what's missing immediately.

Here's the major scale:

C D E F G A B C

And here's the major pentatonic scale:

C D E G A C

There's a good way of remembering what's missing in the C-major pentatonic scale: just keep in mind something that many music students have found amusing over the years and remember to tell yourself there's no F 'n' B.

Here's the major pentatonic in tab. Play it yourself to hear what it sounds like:

C Major Pentatonic

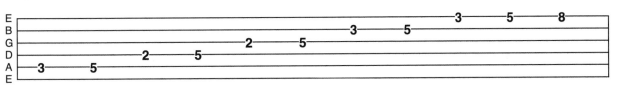

It sounds a little bluesy, perhaps even a little country, if you want to start throwing styles at it. But it's definitely better that you draw your own conclusions.

The Minor Scale

As we saw in the previous chapter, there's no such thing as the definitive minor scale in the way that there is one basic major. To me, the minor scale represents the somewhat confused state that music's been in since things were apparently sorted out just after the Renaissance. Everyone decided on a major scale that summed things up nicely, but when it came to the poor old minor I think they must have adjourned the meeting and gone down the pub. When they got back, the fate of the minor scale didn't seem quite as important as it did previously and so it was left hanging somewhat. The question of which one you should become aurally familiar with is once again down to common usage. One of the minor scales (there are three, incidentally) is known as the *natural minor*, and this is the one we're going to look at first. If you want to extend your scalar capabilities at some point in the future, rest assured that the other two minor scales contain only slight differences. Trust me.

Here's what the natural minor sounds like:

C Natural Minor

▲ Track 18

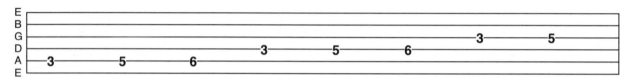

Compare it to the major scale and you should be able to hear that this little fellah sounds a little more subdued than its major counterpart. Feel free to categorise the sound of the minor scale as being sad or whatever comes to mind, as long as the difference between the two is clear in your mind. As I said in the chapter on chords, this is about as important as gender differences, so stay sharp.

The Minor Pentatonic Scale

Once again, this scale can be seen as an abbreviated form of the natural minor. Just to be sure, let's compare the two.

Here's C natural minor:

$$C \quad D \quad E\flat \quad F \quad G \quad A\flat \quad B\flat \quad C$$

And here's C minor pentatonic:

$$C \quad E\flat \quad F \quad G \quad B\flat \quad C$$

Now here's what C minor pentatonic sounds like:

C Minor Pentatonic

▲ Track 19

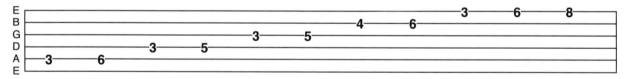

If you think that this sounds bluesy, you'd definitely be on the right track. Add a couple of notes here and there and we're definitely in blues territory (see the chapter on "The Style Mile" for details).

Learning Scales – Stage One

This will depend on how long you've spent with scales so far, really. If you've not spent any time at all, your first step should be to play all of the above about five times each per day, which should ensure that the physical and musical sides of your development begin together. Repetition of these scales will begin to develop your hand and co-ordination skills while actually listening to what you're doing will start the music side off nicely. Now, I can't stress this side of things too much: *remember* to listen to what you're doing. Don't let your mind wander – this is why we repeat each scale only five times, initially, which doesn't give you the time to become bored. When you start to become familiar with the sounds of the scales, hum them while you play them. This will start inputting the music to your head, which is where, ultimately, it will do you the most good.

Playing the above scales five times a day will only take you a couple of minutes, so you can tell yourself that you'll be able to quit way before the boredom factor sets in and get on with something else. Do this for around a month.

Stage Two

After a while, the scales are going to start sounding very predictable, and this is exactly the right time to start extending all of them away from their basic states and into something more functional.

Here's the next stage for the major scale:

C Major

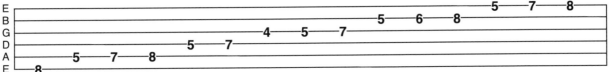

We've now extended it to two octaves, more than half the musical range of the guitar. You'll find yourself presented with a new physical challenge – that of learning a new fingering – and a new musical one, too, in that you've extended your range.

We can also do the same for the natural minor:

C Natural Minor

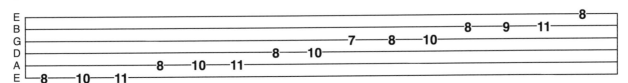

As with the major scale, here you've got a musical extension and another set of fingering to absorb.

However, things change a little when we come to the pentatonic scales. We've started with two-octave scales here, and so the option of actually extending them across the fingerboard isn't available to us. Instead, what we'll do is look at another fingering pattern that can be used for both major and minor pentatonic scales. First, let's have a look at the major:

C Major Pentatonic

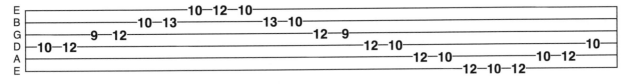

Play the scale using the exact fingering shown above, despite the fact that we might appear to be starting a little way in.

Next, we'll do exactly the same for the minor pentatonic. You've probably already noticed that the shapes for the major and minor pentatonics are the same and that all we appear to be doing is starting on different notes. This is all to do with economy and is one of the rare times when music is actually on our side.

C Minor Pentatonic

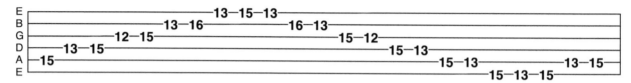

Note: This fingering may be a little awkward if your acoustic doesn't have a cutaway

The practice regime for these scales is very much the same as before: play each of them five times every day. You should find that it takes about the same amount of time as it did when you practised the scales initially, because your technique will have improved to the stage where you can cope with a few extra notes in the same amount of time. Which brings us to another all-important topic…

Timing

Up to this point, I haven't introduced this other dimension of music because I'm aware that there's a lot of initial fumbling around to begin with and that the last thing you want is something else to think about. However, a good sense of timing is absolutely vital if you're going to be able to play anything at all. Timing is one part of other areas of music, such as phrasing, and is the single most ignored part of everyone's practice routine.

What I would advise is that you buy yourself a metronome or a cheap drum machine – anything that's capable of keeping a measured beat going while you practise. To begin with, set the metronome (or whatever) to around 80 beats per minute and play one note per click against it. Just in case you're a bit in the dark about what I mean here, this diagram should sort things out for you. Make sure you play a note on each "1 2 3 4".

|| 1 2 3 4 | 1 2 3 4 | 1 2 3 4 | 1 2 3 4 || (80bpm)

If you find this basic synchronisation irritatingly difficult at first, persevere – it will do you so much good in the long run.

When you've got everything nicely in line, gradually increase the beats per minute on the metronome – and I mean gradually! Don't increase it from 80 to 160 overnight; one stop at a time or around five to ten beats per minute is fine for now.

Stage Three

Hopefully, you've again reached the point where practising scales with a metronome is taking up only the first few minutes of your daily routine. Everything should be rock solid before you allow yourself to progress any further. The scales should all be sounding very familiar to you now and you might even find that you're beginning to hear things on records that are making some kind of sense to you. If so, good; this is a sign that your ear is developing nicely. If not, don't be too concerned, because people's ears develop at different rates. Some take to it straight away while others find it a struggle. The thing to remember is that developing this side of your musicality is invaluable and you should persevere accordingly.

The next stage is pretty much the full monty, as far as the scales we've been looking at are concerned, because we're going to spread all of the scales all over the fretboard.

C Major Scale

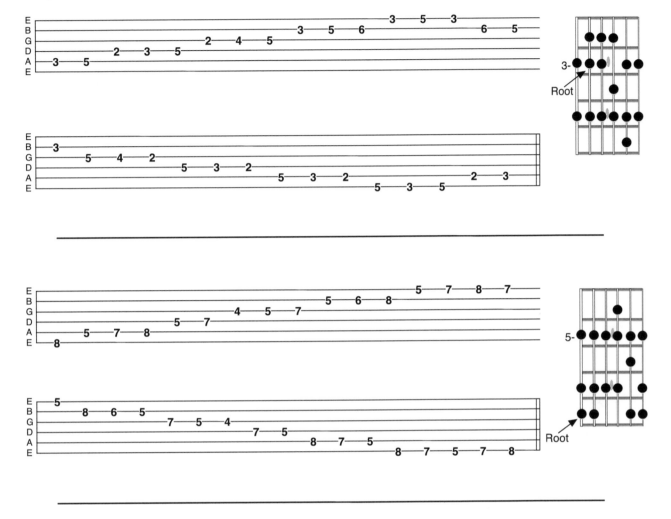

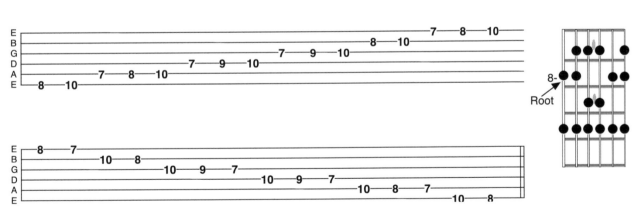

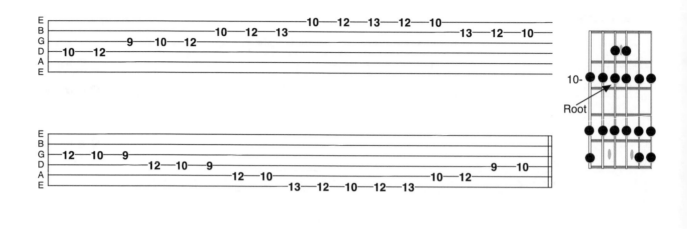

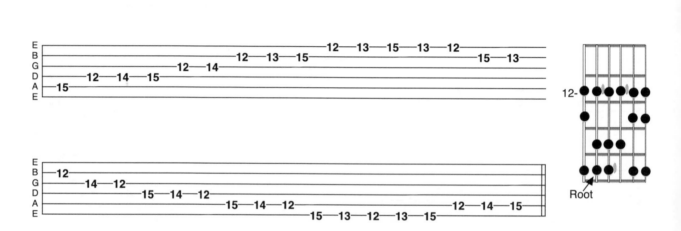

C Natural Minor Scale

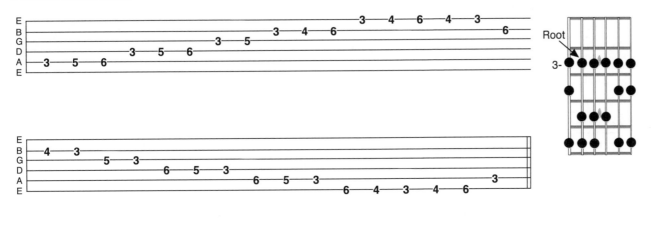

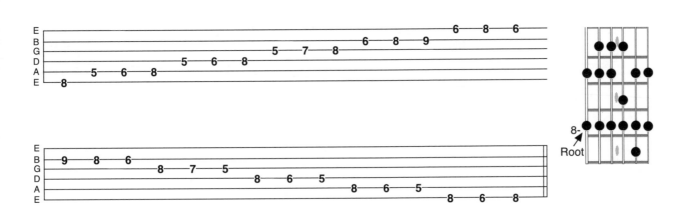

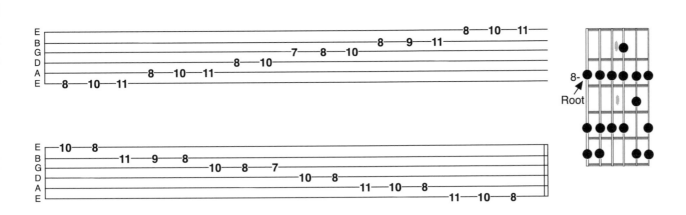

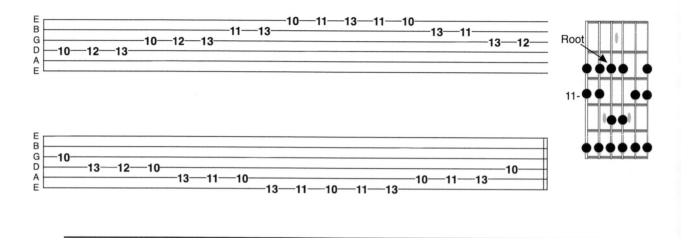

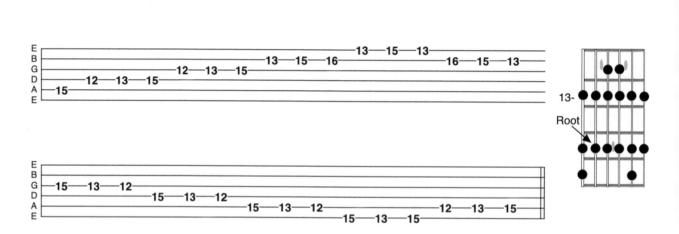

C Major Pentatonic Scale

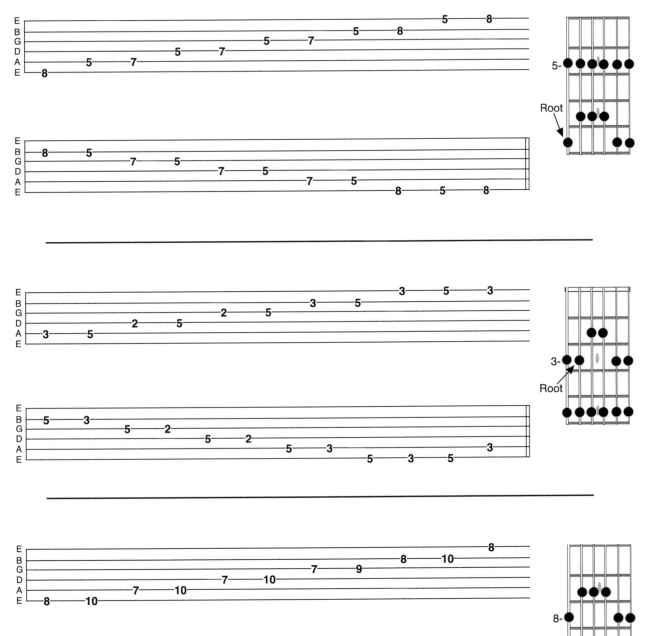

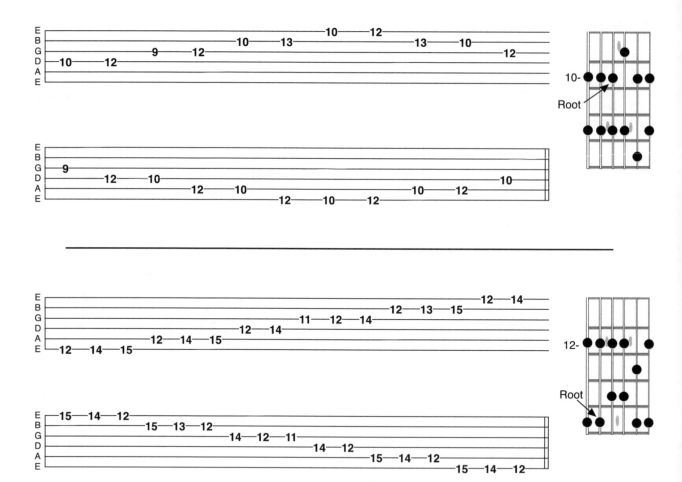

C Minor Pentatonic Scale

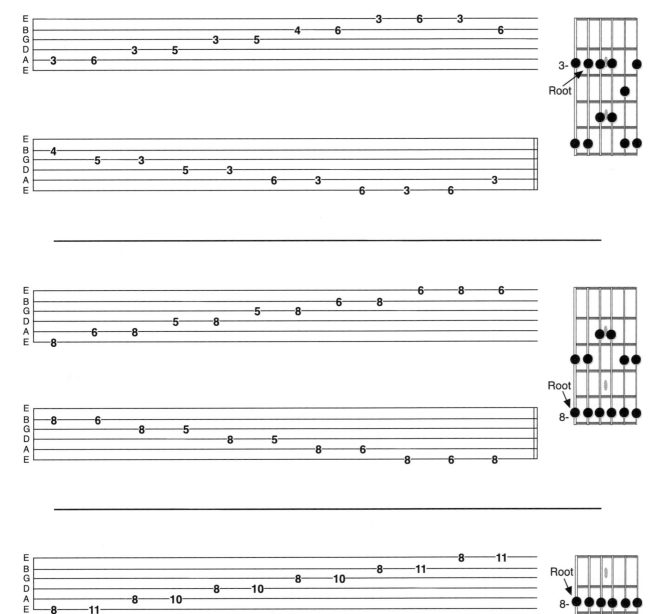

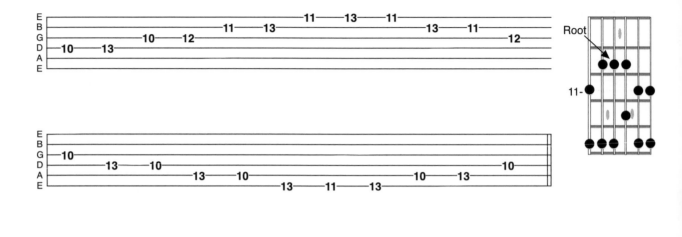

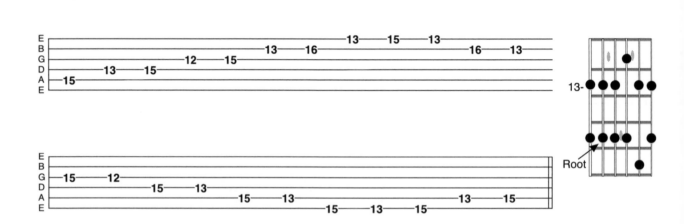

Your scale practice routine is only going to differ fractionally from before. I still don't recommend you spend any longer than just a few minutes daily on scales, as it's important that you don't see practising scales as a chore. Keep the positive thought in your mind that you're developing vital areas of your musical nature and definitely not just wasting time doing some exercises.

Metronome Timings

Once you've reached around 120-140 beats per minute, you'll need to slow things down again and start playing eighth notes on every beat. This isn't hard; it just takes a bit of a rethink. By playing things in the way you've been doing so far, you've been playing quarter notes (or crotchets, if you prefer). That's four beats to the bar, each beat representing a quarter part of that bar – right? Now, you'll need to

play eight notes per bar. The new counting procedure looks like this:

|| 1 & 2 & 3 & 4 & | 1 & 2 & 3 & 4 & | 1 & 2 & 3 & 4 & ||

So that's "one-and-two-and-three-and-four-and" per bar, with a note played on each. Reduce your beats per minute back to 80 and start again with eighth notes, working your way forwards *gradually*.

You don't have to play every scale shape I've given you; instead, restrict your scale practice to a few minutes only by playing a couple of (different) shapes for each type every day.

Stage Four

The next thing to do is change the key of everything you've learned so far. This sounds like a huge task, but it isn't really. The guitar is great for moving things around, and whereas instruments like the clarinet and the piano have a different fingering pattern for each scale in each key, we can keep to the shapes we've already learned and just move them up or down the neck.

As an example of how exactly this trick works, look at this. Here's the familiar shape for C major. (Take note of the circled notes – they're the roots, which in this case are Cs.)

C major

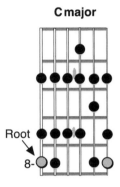

If we wanted to play D♭ major, all we'd have to do is move things up one fret and play the exact same shape.

D♭ major

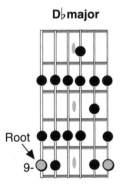

Easy, huh? And we can apply this kind of thinking to every scale we've looked at (and all the ones we haven't). All you need to do is match up the root notes and away you go. In order to do this, you're going to have to draw yourself a neck diagram showing where all the notes are on the first twelve frets of the guitar neck (they start repeating after

that). I want you to do this yourself, because you'll remember it better that way, but as a guide, here are the notes on the bass E string from the open string to the twelfth fret:

E || F | F♯ | G | G♯ | A | B♭ | B | C | C♯ | D | E♭ | E |
open 1   2   3   4   5   6   7   8   9   10   11   12

That's actually given you two strings out of six, the top and bottom Es, and I'll leave it to you to fill in the other four strings on your own.

The next stage is simply to mix and match. If you wanted to play this scale shape…

C Major Pentatonic

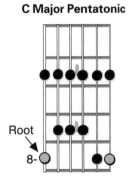

…in the key of B♭, you'd start on fret six of the bass E string. If you wanted to play it in the key of D, you'd start on the tenth. Get the idea?

So now your daily routine will comprise picking a key and taking a few minutes playing the four different scale shapes in that key. It's important for now that you stick to one key for all of the scale shapes, as this will keep feeding their different musical personalities into your head.

Metronome Targets

Your target is to be able to play each of the scales at a moderate-to-fast speed. I'll cover the differences between playing with a pick or pure fingerstyle later on, but just to give you the basic idea…

Once you've gone up to around 120 beats per minute with eighth notes, you'll need to start looking at the next beat division: the 16th note or semiquaver. This entails playing four notes per beat (or metronome click) and would look something like this on paper:

|| 1-e-&-uh 2-e-&-uh 3-e-&-uh 4-e-&-uh ||

(This translates to "one-ee-and-uh", etc.) By playing this pattern, every time the metronome clicks, you're playing four notes. You'll need to wind the metronome down to about 80bpm to begin with, or maybe even 60, and you're going to push it up to only about 100-120. This kind of speed is very difficult with fingers (although flamenco and classical guitar players manage it), so you might find yourself having to make some compromises if fingerstyle is going to be your thing.

Further Study

Once you've got your scales fluent enough to be able to play them fairly fast in any specified key with no mistakes, you'll probably want to move onto the more exotic realms that music has to offer. If you're looking to follow a specific style, check out my recommendations in "The Style Mile", but if you just want to further your scale studies and introduce your ear to some more material then you should buy a scale book – there are quite a few on the market – and look through it. Try everything so you can make your own decisions based on your own musical personality. If you find something that you really think you can use in your music, apply the same rules that have been listed here. And start slowly, gradually building up speed and fluency in every key.

RIGHT-HAND DEVELOPMENT

"My main guitar teacher was very much of the old school, the 1920s/1930s Clifford Essex/BMG school – a multi-instrumentalist banjoist, mandolinist, guitarist. But when I began with him it was fairly obvious to me, at age twelve or 13, that there was a gap: the right hand hadn't actually been addressed. Arch-wrist is more banjo, and you'll also find it a lot in mandolin picking, which is probably one of the very few codified approaches to a pick, funnily enough. Follow-through mandolin picking would now be probably considered quaint." Robert Fripp

The first decision you have to make when it comes to the right hand is whether you're going to play purely fingerstyle or use a pick. For the time being, I'm going to put aside any considerations like hybrid picking where a combination of the two is employed; I'm talking here about the right way to start down either of the two major roads open to you. It's difficult to pinpoint the advantages and disadvantages of either system – it's really a bit of give and take on both sides. Stylistically, it's pretty much an open book, but we can consider a few pointers.

Logically speaking, if you're going to end up playing with a plectrum, you have to consider the various styles of acoustic-guitar accompaniment and how these might have to be adapted. Certainly, an arpeggiated style (ie playing chords one string at a time) places quite a high demand on the picking arm, whereas fingers have approximately four times the chance of being able to cope (ie you've got four fingers as opposed to one pick). However, a plastic pick sounds entirely different to soft flesh on the strings and, in general, sounds better for melodic playing (or playing guitar solos, if you prefer).

So how do you choose? My advice is to try both, because most players find that they're drawn towards one or the other fairly soon and the minute a style starts to form, you usually find you're set that way for life.

Incidentally, I'm not ignoring the fact that a lot of very great players have elected to play using fingerpicks, thumbpicks or a combination of the two – to me, that's a modified form of fingerpicking, that's all. It's the same if a player ends up playing with hybrid picking – it's a variation on fingerpicking. When I talk about playing with a pick, I mean solely a pick.

Here's an excerpt from an interview I conducted with John Hammond:

DM: Where did the idea to use fingerpicks come from?

JH: Well, I saw Dave Van Ronk play in the Village in '61 and I saw that he used fingerpicks. I'd just begun to play guitar and I thought that a thumb pick seemed to make it so much louder. The fingerpick was a little harder to get used to, but I was driven at that point to get it down, and so it all came together.

DM: Do you use mainly upstrokes with the fingerpick?

JH: Yes.

DM: So it's almost like a conventional fingerstyle with the fingerpicks added?

JH: Exactly.

The Plectrum

"If someone comes to you or me or someone else for guitar lessons and they say, 'Come on then, show me how to hold a pick,' what they are actually saying is, 'Show me how to lead my life.' But that's often not what they believe is the question that is being asked." *Robert Fripp*

I'd say that most acoustic players tend to shun the plectrum in favour of good old-fashioned flesh or fingernails. I don't know what it is, although I've heard many players talk about flesh being more "real" than plastic. So, if you chose the plastic route, you may well be in the minority, but that shouldn't put you off. Like I say, try both and see which feels more natural.

"Because I play with my thumb, I lose a lot of attack. We're talking about the difference between flesh or plastic on steel." *Jim Mullen*

To begin with, a word or two about picks in general. Be aware that they come in all shapes, sizes, materials, weights and so on, so you're best off buying a variety at first and finding out which feels more comfortable. As a rough guide, the lighter plectrums (say .44mm) are better for strumming chords – a purely rhythmic approach – whereas the heavier ones (say 1mm) are better for single-note work. The exact choice of shape or material I'll leave up to you. The truth is that players get themselves into all kinds of habits where picks are concerned. Jazz virtuoso Joe Pass used to use a pick broken in half when he played, confessing that he couldn't remember why he started doing it, that it was just something he always did. Then again, some players opt for tiny picks (these used to be called *mandolin picks*) while others choose huge great kite-shaped objects (this would include Buddy Guy, incidentally).

"I use copper picks… Engineers like them for their acoustic tone. They have a very warm quality, unlike other metal picks, which are very cold." *Jerry Donahue*

Holding a pick is straightforward enough: hold it between your index finger and your thumb, letting the rest of the hand relax. In general, don't form a fist with the fingers not involved in holding the pick as this introduces tension into the hand and tension is one of the guitar player's worst enemies.

Be careful not to "dig in" too deep with the pick, especially when playing chords. Use only the tip of the pick – roughly the top 2mm – or you'll be making lifting movements with your wrist between each string stroke, which will slow you down.

Once you're comfortable with holding the pick, take a few moments to check out your wrist action. There shouldn't be any tension present in this part of your anatomy at all – you're not breaking rocks here, you're playing a musical instrument, so you should try to rid your wrist of any unwarranted tension right from the start.

I suppose that playing with a plectrum can be split into two main areas: playing chords and playing single notes. We'll look at chords first. (Incidentally, by playing chords, I mean strumming as opposed to arpeggiating, or playing a chord one note at a time.)

Strumming Patterns

"Even though you're into guitar and you want to be able to do all these fancy things and get to a point of capability, I think it's really important not to ignore songwriting and basic rhythm playing and the simplicity of it, the beauty of a simple chord change. If you can get that together while you're learning and while you're developing, you'll end up a lot more brilliant in the end." *Nuno Bettencourt*

This area of playing is all to do with rhythm, as it's probably the most recognised form of song accompaniment. As such, we'd better lay down some ground rules right from the start. Let's take a few bars of a song and look at them purely from a rhythmical point of view. The most common form of rhythm is 4/4 and is shown as a fraction at the beginning of a piece of music. A piece in 4/4 means that it has four beats to the bar, like this:

‖ 1 2 3 4 | 1 2 3 4 | 1 2 3 4 | 1 2 3 4 ‖

Initially, try playing this with a downstroke of the pick on every beat (a downstroke is played by strumming down towards the floor – assuming that you're not playing with your feet in the air). Count along out loud as you do so, trying to make sure that everything is moving to a regular beat. If you have a metronome (and I did recommend a while ago that you should buy one), set it to about 80 beats per minute and play along with that, counting out loud "one, two, three, four" as you do.

The self-conscious among you might fight shy of actually counting out loud, but even this small thing does you a lot of good as it means that you focus on the timing. You won't have to do it forever as rhythm eventually becomes part of your subconscious array of musical abilities. Another tip is to tap your foot in time with the metronome as you play. This literally teaches you to "feel" rhythm, something that's vitally important to your musical development.

After trying downstrokes at various speeds for a while, you'll need to start introducing upstrokes into your rhythm technique. If you try a couple of experimental upstrokes, you'll be able to hear how they differ in sound from downstrokes. One of the reasons why this should be so is that upstrokes tend to be "lighter" than downstrokes – you don't have gravity on your side, for a start. So a mixture of down- and upstrokes will provide a natural texture to an accompaniment without too much effort at all. Having said that, however, it's got to be organised…

One of the ways in which we can use the change in dynamic between up- and downstrokes is to organise things so that upstrokes are used on the "lighter" side of the beat. Take a bar of 4/4, this time split into eighth notes:

|| 1 & 2 & 3 & 4 & | 1 & 2 & 3 & 4 & ||

This time, you'd be counting out loud, saying, "One and two and three and four and" and your upstrokes would all fall on the ands. It's going to sound a little military at first, a little like a clockwork toy, but don't worry about this because we're soon going to loosen things up.

At this point, I must add that I've seen all sorts of different approaches to picking (or, indeed, strumming)

work, and some of them are dangerously haphazard, to say the least, so beware of the quirk factor in association with strumming technique as you'll probably see some wild things happening in this respect on TV or video. I've always taken the attitude that it's best to start off with a very formal approach to rhythm and, once the basics have been established, to let students develop their own little idiosyncrasies in terms of rhythm style. Don't worry if this approach feels a little heavy-handed at first – it really is important to establish the fundamentals before trying anything too awkward.

To begin with, use either four-to-the-bar downstrokes or eighth-note up-and-down strumming to play through songs, trying to keep everything flowing evenly. Use a metronome and tap your foot, counting out loud as you go.

The next stage to look at is 16th-note rhythm. Now, this doesn't crop up too often, as it begins to sound far too cluttered if the basic metre of a song is anything over 100 beats per minute (unless, of course, you're Pete Townshend), so taking a whole bar of 16th notes is probably a little extreme, and you won't often see it out in the field, but we're dealing with theoretics here.

| 1-e-&-uh 2-e-&-uh 3-e-&-uh 4-e-&-uh |

As far as up- and downstrokes are concerned, with 16th notes it's best to remain strictly alternate. This aids the natural flow and, of course, it means that you always end up with a nice strong downstroke on the first part of every beat. This is a very important part of marking time as, if you're playing without any other kind of rhythm instrument (ie a drummer), the job of outlining the rhythm is down to you. If in doubt, always go back to basics and play things four to the bar as downstrokes, adding the other fractional parts of the beat later on.

As far as straightforward rhythm playing is concerned, things don't actually get much more complicated than this. When you think about it, you can't really be expected to keep a 32nd-note rhythm going, as it would be a bit of a blur. In fact, we go in absolutely the opposite direction and start missing out beats or mixing and matching 16th-, eighth- and quarter-note rhythms to make up some interesting accompaniment ideas. Look at this:

| 1 & 2 & 3-e-&-uh 4 & |

That's a fairly good example of what I mean. You can probably imagine just how many variations there are available by simply combining the three rhythmic elements that we've looked at so far – or, at least, I hope you can, because that's a bit of homework to do, just mixing up some of the things we've looked at so far and playing along with a metronome. The vital thing is to make sure that everything you do is metrically correct and that the basic 4/4 rhythm is outlined perfectly. Continue to test yourself in this way until you can't trip yourself up at all. This will mean that your sense of rhythm is developing nicely.

Invisible Rhythm

"Rhythmically, I can remember things, and that's only because I had good teachers. I don't think that I have any superhuman gift for it." *Joe Satriani*

You might have heard about rests in music. Musically speaking, these are used to indicate a spot where nothing actually happens at all on a beat or beats. You could have a situation where you were expected to play on the first beat of the bar but nothing would actually go on for the other three beats, something like this:

| 1 (2) (3) (4) | 1 (2) (3) (4) |

or:

| (1) 2 (3) 4 | (1) 2 (3) 4 |

The beats in brackets are where the rests fall – don't play anything here at all.

All of this might appear very easy – it's much less vigorous than playing 16th notes on every beat, at any rate – but leaving things out can sometimes be surprisingly difficult. The problem here is to make sure that everything doesn't fall apart and that the beats where you do play fall exactly where they should. Try it – you should be able to see what I mean. Getting used to the idea of invisible rhythm will be much easier if you've got a metronome or drum machine chugging away in the background while you count yourself through the silent beats, and this is something I would definitely advise you to use, at least until your inner sense of rhythmic awareness has developed to the point at which you can play this sort of thing in your sleep.

Remember that, even when beats are rested, your upstroke and downstroke routine should still remain intact, and here you should still land squarely on the beat with a downstroke on the strong parts of the bar. In this way, it's a good thing to keep the wrist going up and down, even when you're not playing anything during part of a bar – it's a sure-fire way of making sure that all of the ups and downs happen where they should.

This idea of using "phantom pickstrokes" is highlighted when parts of eighth- or 16th-note patterns are rested. Look at this:

| 1-(e-&)-uh 2-(e-&)-uh 3-(e-&)-uh 4-(e-&)-uh |

Looks like a complete nightmare, doesn't it? But it's not if you keep your wrist moving, making phantom pickstrokes in time with the 16th-note pattern, miming the beats that aren't rested. Eventually, you'll find that you can probably rid yourself of the phantom element altogether; your wrist will know instinctively which part of the beat it's required to play and whether it's an up- or a downstroke. So, in many respects, the busier things are at first, the sooner all of the spadework will be done and you'll be finding yourself with a nicely developed and economical picking style.

As I've said, the number of variations available to you by employing just these relatively simple rhythmic ideas is very great indeed and should see you through most domestic situations, as far as accompaniment is concerned. But you don't just want to strum chords all the time, do you? It might be nice to mix everything up even more, play individual notes and arpeggios, too, and make up a fully rounded right-hand picking style.

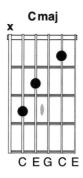

Arpeggios

The word *arpeggio* means "harp-like", but to you and me it means playing chords one note at a time as an alternative to playing them simultaneously. It's an attractive accompaniment style and isn't too difficult to master.

Effectively, there are two ways that you can go about playing arpeggios with a pick. The first is almost like a slow strum – ie you play all the notes of a chord one after the other using a continuous downstroke or upstroke (there are some examples of this on the CD). The only real difference is that you're trying to give each note of the chord its individual space instead of blurring everything together.

The other way of playing arpeggios is to treat each note as an individual up- or downstroke. When you're playing in this particular style, you'll still be expected to keep time, and so this kind of playing is really only an extension of what we've already looked at above.

In order to start becoming familiar with playing arpeggios with a pick, take a few of the straightforward chord shapes and experiment with picking each note individually. Let's take a C-major chord:

C maj

x

C E G C E

Take things slowly at first, remembering the Three Ps – Patience, Persistence and Practice. Try to give each note an equal dynamic, as opposed to acknowledging the strong and weak parts of the beat, as we did earlier. Play it both ways, soft and loud – this will help you out in the long run, as guitar parts that call for arpeggios often have their own individual inner dynamics.

Obviously, the next step is to extend the idea of arpeggiating chords to all of the chords in your vocabulary. Literally take a few minutes each practice period to spend some time employing this technique. It will gradually become second nature.

Single Notes

When you're playing single notes, phrases, licks, scales or whatever, the recommended regime with the plectrum is *alternate picking*. This involves playing a downstroke followed by an upstroke on consecutive notes. So, if you check out the chapter on "Painless Music Theory II – Scales" and choose to play a scale of C major using a pick, you'd start with a downstroke on the C and continue with an upstroke on the D and so on.

Alternate picking is a method that has existed for years and has achieved some considerable degree of acceptability in the eyes of teachers internationally. In practice, of course, the occasional consecutive series of down- or upstrokes creeps into everyday playing, and the good old quirk factor means that videos and live performances are positively awash with variations on the alternate-picking theme. This, of course, is all well and good – certain passages are easier to play this way, after all – but it's good to get into the habit and discipline of alternate picking before you allow yourself to break the rules.

The piece that you're about to hear will need a fair amount of strict alternate picking, so be prepared for something of a workout.

The Graduation Piece

Sometimes, I find myself resorting to some very old-fashioned ideas to help solve contemporary problems, and picking scales and arpeggios is a case in point. In fact, we're going to look at a piece by a composer called Matteo Carcassi (1792-1853) to help us play with a pick. In his time, Carcassi wrote a great number of pieces for guitar, many of which were intended to improve specific techniques. Naturally, you don't need me to tell you that he didn't exactly think we'd be playing them on metal strings and using a pick, but I'm sure he'd be chuffed to think that they were still very much in use. (Of course, it's tempting to believe that the plectrum is a modern addition to guitar playing, but in fact a lot of Baroque guitar from around the 17th century was played using picks made from metal or quills.)

It's not surprising to find that we can apply 200-year-old solutions to modern-day guitar-playing problems in this way. After all, the problems themselves haven't really changed that much – at least, in terms of developing technique they haven't.

This piece is the first of a series of 25 that Carcassi wrote under the general title of "Melodic Studies" and it looks specifically at playing simple scale and arpeggio ideas. I've modified it so that it works with a pick, but I haven't actually taken that much away. It's pretty much the same as it was 200 years ago.

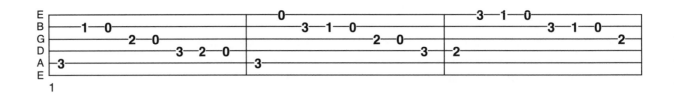

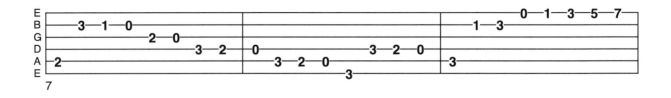

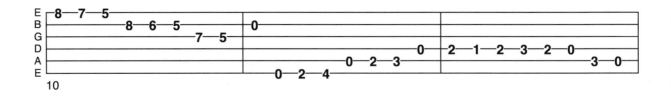

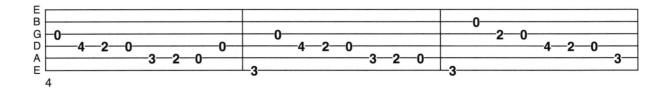

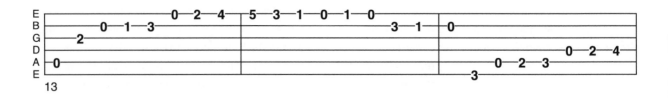

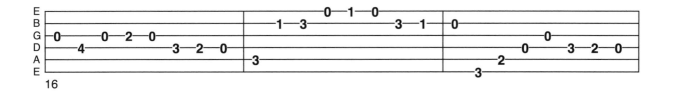

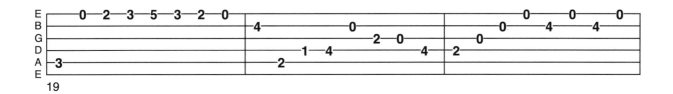

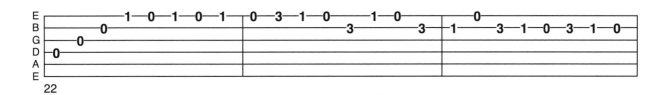

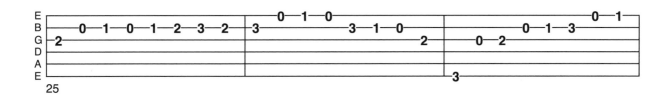

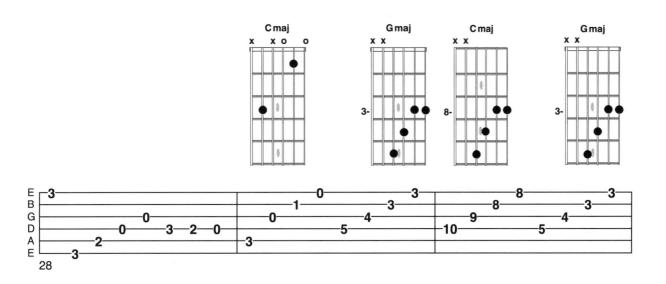

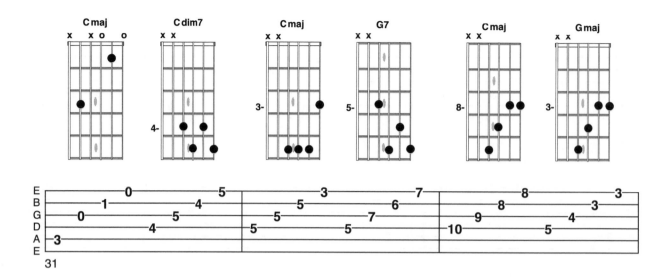

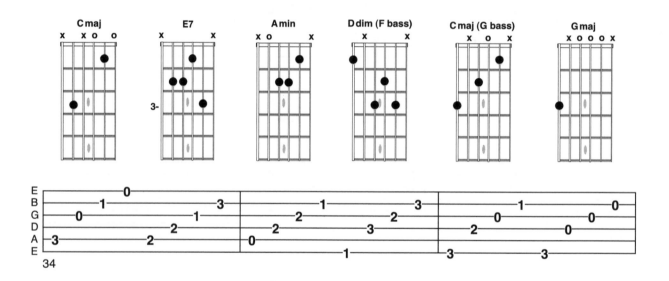

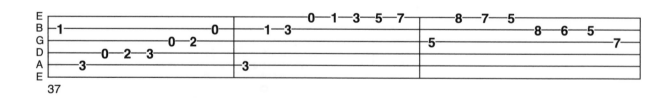

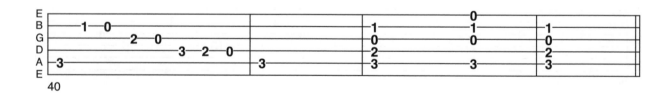

After playing through this particular piece, you should find that you're ready for just about anything. However, if you want to add yet more versatility to your right hand's performance, my advice is to have a go at playing fingerstyle, too.

Fingerstyle Basics

"I used to borrow acoustic guitars and ended up learning fingerstyle." *Mark Knopfler*

When we talk about players using their right-hand fingers instead of a pick, it might be that the first image that springs to mind is that of the humble folk guitarist, but that's very much an image from the past. Nowadays, fingerstyle has a place in many different forms of guitar playing. Just think of a few of these names: Mark Knopfler, Jeff Beck, Pierre Bensusan, John Williams, Juan Martin, Colin Reid. That covers a pretty wide stylistic area, doesn't it?

As King Crimson's Robert Fripp says, despite all the rock, pop and jazz tutors that exist in the world, there has never really been an orthodoxy established for the right hand. No one's ever come out and said, "This is the right way." All we've had to go on are the similarities between classical and "popular" guitar technique, in this respect. Now, hopefully, we're about to put that right.

Initially, we're going to be looking at the rights and wrongs of right-hand positioning and how to ensure that your fingers have the best possible chance of working at maximum efficiency. After all, playing the guitar well is a difficult enough job in itself. We don't want to make things unnecessarily hard for ourselves, do we?

"If you want to take it seriously, learning to play classical is a bit of a serious discipline and you can't really mix it. It taught me to use my right hand and you get to hear and play some lovely music. I think that you get something out of any musical education. I certainly got a lot out of it." *Robbie McIntosh*

Flesh Or Nails?

Here's a debate that raged like an inferno at one time in classical guitar: do you sound the strings using the right-hand fingernails or flesh? Eventually, I believe the matter was resolved and, in general, nails won. In actual fact, it tends to be a combination of both, as the string travels across the flesh of the fingertip before being finally sounded by the nail at the end of its journey.

As you might think, this tends to cause a lot of wear and tear on the fingernails, and anyone who has ever known a classical-playing professional will know just how much care and attention his manicure receives. I spent a while playing classical in wine bars and the like and I was never seen without a piece of .00-grade wet-and-dry paper and an emery board for the almost continuous maintenance required by my fingernails. Of course, this was playing on relatively soft nylon strings, where we're now talking about the far more abrasive metal string.

Acoustic strings can do an awful lot of damage to your fingernails and we're lucky that acoustic players as a breed aren't half as precious about their nails as their classical counterparts have to be. On classical guitar, a lot of your tone lies in the exact manner in which the guitar string is sounded, and in this respect nails can make a tremendous difference. As far as a nylon-string guitar is concerned, having a bad nail day is a serious nightmare. I was once due to play a gig at a Masonic hall and I managed to break a nail 30 minutes before leaving home to go to the gig. (I broke it drawing a curtain, so it wasn't as if I was doing anything frivolous.) I found myself having to glue the nail back in place, and not every glue works on fingernails. I know of a flamenco player who has glue specially imported from Spain for the purpose of fingernail emergencies!

Metal-string fingerstylists are known to take some measured precautions as far as their nails are concerned. It's not uncommon to use a clear lacquer on the nails of the right hand to provide additional strength. (Check with your mum/girlfriend before borrowing any, though, won't you? It can give an entirely wrong impression.) There are also various remedies for weak nails on the market that are all worth exploring if you find yourself wanting to play in this way. The bottom line is that everyone is different. I'm lucky in that I have a set of talons for fingernails, and so metal strings don't manage to do much damage. (You might be asking yourself how it was that

I managed to break a nail drawing a curtain. Believe it or not, I'm still trying to work that one out myself!)

My advice would be to try both flesh and fingernails and then make your mind up as to which method sounds better. The bottom line is that flesh is soft while nails are sort of built-in plectrums, and you'll hear a real difference between the two.

Naming The Fingers

One of the more helpful things that classical technique can bestow upon us is the convention for naming the right-hand fingers. It's not really been necessary to invent another one, as things seem to run quite smoothly with the accepted convention in place. So here's what we've got:

Thumb = p
Index = i
Middle = m
Ring = a

You might have already guessed that these lower-case letters represent the Spanish names for the fingers and aren't just random letters. If you've ever scanned across some classical guitar music, you'll have come across this lettering convention before. It can certainly lead to some amusing spellings above certain passages. I kept a careful eye on things like this when I was teaching (it was my way of trying to retain a sense of humour) and the most original spelling I came up with was "im a miami pimp". This purely accidental confession indicated that the right-hand fingering convention for the piece of music in question called on the performer to use index, middle, ring, middle, index, ring and so on. Well, it made me laugh.

Right-Hand Position With A Twist

One of the first and most basic rules about right-hand position is that you should try to eliminate tension in forearm, wrist, hand and fingers almost totally. Tensing up is your worst enemy for two main reasons: it decreases the hand's efficiency and it places you in danger of succumbing to an RSI-type complaint. We've all heard of tendonitis – inflammation of the tendon – and it really is something that you want to

try to avoid, as the only real cure is to stop playing for a while. So the best plan is to adopt a right-hand position that will give your hand maximum flexibility and keep you out of Casualty at the same time, right?

"Characters who come to me with problems with their hands find that it is often to do with tension." *Robert Fripp*

The following pictures show a variety of hand positions that I've come across from either teaching or freeze-framing videos (who said that guitar teaching doesn't get sad occasionally?). The first one I'd draw your attention to is the first picture, which is as good a place to start as any.

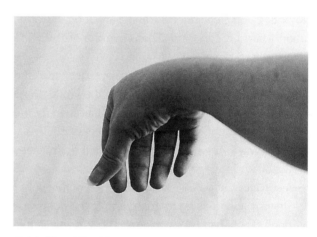

Basic Hand Position

The main thing to look at is the fact that the fingers are almost straight and not cramped or curled up. The other thing to note is that the index finger and thumb form an X. The reason for adopting this shape is simple: it keeps these two digits out of each other's way. If you think about it, the index finger is moving inwards towards the palm as it follows through after plucking the string while the thumb moves downwards, and the possibilities for collision and near misses would give an air-traffic controller nightmares, so it's important to try to adopt a convention that will keep them apart when in action.

"[In] the early '60s, [when] folk was still very much the thing…I didn't know how to fingerpick.

I tried to work it out myself and did things like copying a recording by Jack Elliot without realising that he was a flatpicker! But I learned by watching other people and by talking to them – Tony McPhee taught me how to tune the guitar in an open tuning for slide, for instance. But I used to watch how people used their fingers, and I still use my fingers in preference to using a pick. I used a thumb pick for a while, but I find that using my fingers gives me more control and makes everything more sensitive." *Dave Kelly, The Blues Band*

Now take a look at this picture showing that finger/hand position transferred to the guitar strings:

Correct Hand Position

This is the classical position for a hand "at rest" on the guitar strings. Once again, convention decrees that the fingers are very loosely assigned strings. (I say loosely because it's impossible to have too rigid a rule here, as different fingerings will inevitably break every rule in the book, eventually.) So position your hand thus: the index finger (i) on the G string, the middle finger (m) on the B and the ring finger (a) on the top E. The thumb looks after the bass strings. Keep the fingers as straight as possible and don't let the wrist collapse, but don't arch it quite as high as I did for this picture! Merely waggling your fingers around will tell you that there's a lot of movement possible – and if a few of you are muttering to yourselves, "What about muting the strings?", don't worry, we'll get there.

Bad Positions

A common fault that students new to fingerstyle make is to try to anchor their hands to the bodies of their guitars in some way. Look at the picture below – here I've allowed one of my fingers to touch the guitar. I guess it's all to do with feeling a little insecure about allowing your fingers to touch only the strings. The consensus decrees that, if you're touching the body, you've got a little more control, but technically you're limiting the flexibility of the hand in general and you're losing the use of a finger.

Anchored Finger – Wrong!

Worse still is the following example. Here, a couple of fingers have attached themselves to the guitar, resulting in even less tension-free movement and fewer fingers to play with.

Two Fingers Anchored – Wrong!

The next example is quite common, especially with beginners. To overcome the feeling that you're either going to drop the guitar altogether or it's going to fall from your lap, many people try to hold the guitar up by adopting this crippling hand position. What have you got left? A single finger and a thumb – a singular waste of resources if ever I saw one.

Holding Up The Guitar – Wrong!

The other crime against freedom of movement is summed up in the next picture. The wrist has collapsed, the fingers are all curled up and any serious amount of flexibility is lost completely.

Collapsed Wrist – Wrong!

But here's the twist: I've seen all of these so-called "bad" positions work! Martin Taylor anchors one of his fingers to his scratchplate, Mark Knopfler anchors two of his fingers to the face of his Strat while Wes Montgomery and Jim Mullen both attach their fingers to the lower parts of their guitars (as in Picture 5 above) and use their thumbs – and no one's going to tell me that any of these players is not a master of his own particular style.

"I was very fortunate that I always had a very good ear. I've never had any actual musical training, and so I had to hear it and figure it out that way. There was nobody around to explain it to me, and that's the reason I play with my thumb. If there had been a teacher around then, he would have said not to do that! But because there was nobody around to tell me otherwise, the habit stuck." *Jim Mullen*

So I'm asking you to trust me when I say that it's really best to adopt the position shown in Picture 1 as the default for your hand because it really is the one that will offer your right hand the best possible chance of putting together a solid fingerstyle technique. Maybe later on you can customise it, but for now we'll start off following the rules.

Practical Work

Now we come to the exercises. Think of this initial foray into the world of fingerpicking as orienteering – it's just so you can get your fingers used to sitting on the strings.

To begin with, adopt the finger position I spoke of a moment ago: thumb on the A, index on the G, middle on the B and ring on the top E and play the open strings, as shown in Exercise 1.

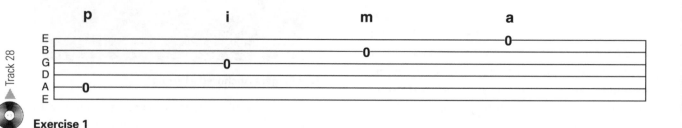

Exercise 1

Track 28

Exercise 2 is the same but in reverse – after the thumb plays, it's the top E string to be played first.

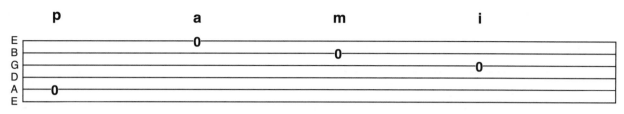

Exercise 2

Neither of the above examples are particularly musical, but it's a good thing to get them both up and running before giving the left hand anything to do. This will give your right hand all the attention it needs at this stage.

Once you've got Exercises 1 and 2 running smoothly, take a look at Exercises 3 and 4. These are based on a C-major chord – nothing too demanding – but playing these will make things sound a little prettier.

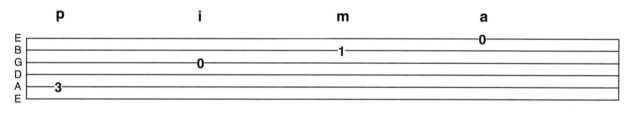

Exercise 3

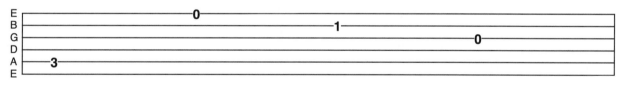

Exercise 4

Exercises 3 and 4 are both essentially repeats of the first two, but they're a lot more musical.

Exercise 5 combines the two previous exercises into one single movement – you're going over and back

again. Take your time with this and don't accept any sloppy playing – it's got to flow evenly. If you have any problems, slow the exercise right down and try playing with a metronome to keep in check rhythmically.

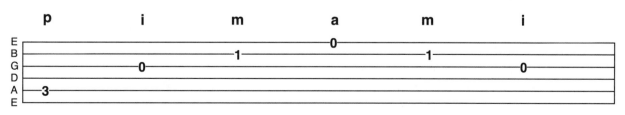

Exercise 5

Exercises 6 and 7 throw another twist into the plot. This time, the thumb alternates between the A and D strings while the fingers carry out the work that they've performed before. If these exercises tie you in knots, take your time, practise them in short bursts so that you don't get frustrated and, above all, have patience.

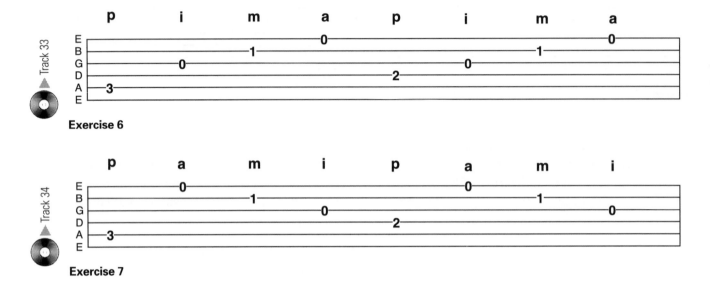

Exercise 6

Exercise 7

A word of caution for these and, for that matter, any of the exercises in this book: if at any time you detect any discomfort in your wrist, fingers or hand, stop playing for a while and let the hand rest. After all, it is learning new tricks, and you're bound to feel a bit of resistance from muscles, tendons and the like, but don't overdo it.

"I went from Scotty Moore to Chet Atkins, and I guess that was where I learned my right-hand fingerpicking technique. In addition, I had a healthy dose of The Ventures and Wes Montgomery along the way, too, and then I started getting into Delta blues. Once I heard Robert Johnson, and that inspired me to combine his style with Chet Atkins' fingerstyle. I put the two together and that was a big step for me." *Sonny Landreth*

A Daily Fingerstyle Workout

Here's a practice routine that will ensure that your fingers continue to develop and generally become able to cope with anything thrown at them. This isn't a one-off set of exercises; I want you to do this little workout every day. It should take you only a couple of minutes, but you can rest assured that you'll be doing your fingers a lot of good in the process. At the very least, it will prove to be an excellent way of warming up your fingers before you start to play anything else. Just look at it as an investment for the future.

The Exercises

Despite the fact that I want you to play all six of these exercises continuously as a single routine, you're going to have to look at them individually at first in order to learn them. I've written them out to be played on a C-major chord, which means that things won't sound too interesting, but they're designed to give you the maximum potential for improving the mobility of your right hand. You could play all of these exercises on open strings, but that really wouldn't sound too good. So, taking them one at a time…

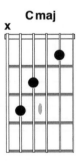

C maj

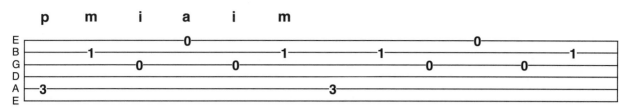

Exercise 8

To begin with, all you're doing is alternating the three fingers and thumb, just to set everything in action. Make sure all the strings are ringing and not muted or muffled in any way.

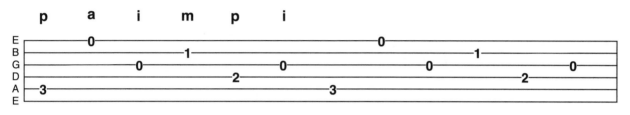

Exercise 9

This exercise is another mix of fingering to bring all of the fingers into play once again, but this time arranged in a different order. Pretty cunning, wouldn't you say?

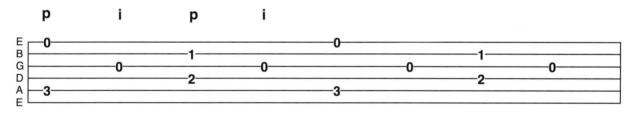

Exercise 10

Now we're playing two notes at once at the beginning and middle of this exercise. Try to make sure that both notes sound equal in volume and try not to "claw" the notes. Remember how you set up the basic right-hand position to be relaxed and not anchored in any way to the guitar body? You should aim to be moving the fingers only, with the minimum amount of tension in the hand itself.

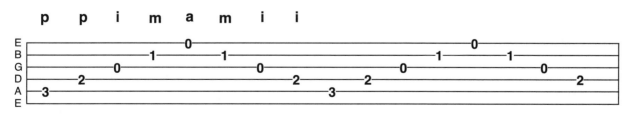

Exercise 11

This exercise is a tricky one; it's a bit like a tongue-twister. It calls for all five notes of the C chord to be played using the four fingers of the right hand. You don't need to be a super mathematician to know that five into four doesn't go, and so we have to adopt some sort of plan to make things flow smoothly. I've borrowed this idea from my classical years and it really does work, if you're patient enough to hang in there and practise it.

Basically, on the way "up" from the chord's bass, the thumb is playing both the fifth and fourth strings and the other fingers are plucking their corresponding strings. On the way back "down", however, the index finger plays both the third and fourth strings. I'm asking you to trust me here; this really does sound a lot smoother than the alternative of having the thumb play the fourth string on both occasions and it's worth practising up from that point of view alone.

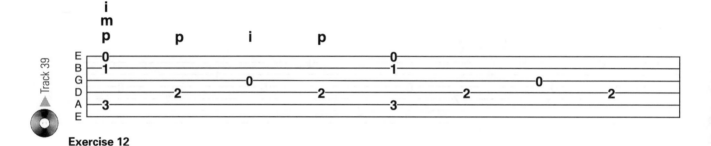

Exercise 12

This is a far gentler exercise, calling for three notes to be played together and a simple alternation with the other fingers. Its position in the practice routine is to give you a bit of a breather after Exercise 11!

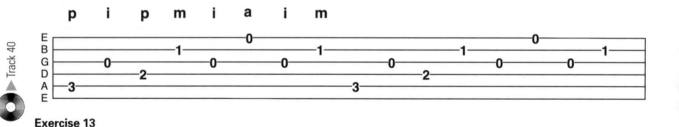

Exercise 13

This is a bit of a twister which finds the fingers playing the notes of the C chord alternately and marks the climactic conclusion to this mini-workout.

The Bells, The Bells

Once you've ironed out any minor problems with each individual exercise, put them all together (in the above order) and repeat each of them about five times. Start off slowly, using a metronome to keep your rhythm in check, and build up the speed gradually. Remember that the full benefit of these exercises will only be felt if the routine is repeated daily over a period of weeks.

The effect of this group of exercises, when played in full, should be like a changing peal of bells, if you'll forgive me for coming over all campanologist with you.

"My style of guitar playing has developed to a point where I'm very good at accompanying myself. I play a unique style, but the only other person I've seen who uses a similar style is Jeff Beck. One night we sat around and we were both trading licks on guitars and I was amazed at what a damn good flatpicker he is.

I'd only ever heard him play electric, but he was tremendous. Then I worked with Andy Summers who, in his spare time, would go to the Munich Philharmonic and play classical guitar. He's a brilliant musician." *Tim Rose*

Playing Melody

Hopefully, you'll keep the above set of exercises as part of your practice routine for some time to come. Playing them will keep on doing you good and make sure that you retain the edge necessary for playing in that particular style.

So much for playing chord-based things – what about individual notes? I mean, where's the melody in all of this? You're definitely going to need a picking regime that works for single notes, too, and once again it's time to plunge into one of guitar playing's grey areas.

As far as fingerstyle guitar is concerned, I've never seen a method for playing melody lines that works. It tends to be a rather haphazard affair, with the guitarist using any fingers that happen to be available. That's fine, but it means that every piece tends to be very non-systematic. In my opinion, it's far better to have a solid system in place that will set you off on the right foot (or finger) every time.

Once again, we find the answer to our demands for a system in the field of classical guitar, in which right-hand fingering is almost 100 per cent more disciplined than in any other field of guitar playing. We borrowed a few ideas from classical guitar when we looked at using a pick, and I hope you agree that it's a pretty fail-safe system and that it lends itself to steel strings very well. Now we're going to do the same thing with playing melody. I'll mention here and now that this is a system that you can alter and adapt to suit your style, but it's a far better place to start than the rather random "any convenient finger" method.

In order to play melody lines on classical guitar, we use a system whereby the fingers of the right hand are alternated – for instance, you would play a simple line using your index finger on the first note, middle finger on the second and back to index for the third, and so on. When this system is explored fully, the ring finger is brought in on the regime as well, but the index and middle fingers are good enough for now.

The Exercises

If you look at Exercise 14, you'll see that all you're doing is playing the first four notes on the top E string up and down. The right-hand fingering starts with the index finger playing the open E string, then the middle finger plays the F on the first fret and so on. You might find this a bit of a finger-twister to begin with, but here's a tip: if you say which finger is next in line out loud (away from family members, or this time they'll throw away the key), it really does help you to keep track. You won't have to do this for long, because it will soon become second nature to you.

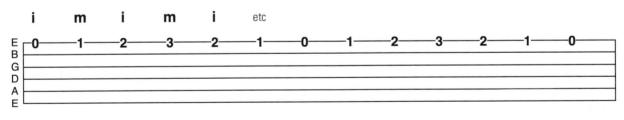

Exercise 14

Exercise 15 is simply an extension of the first idea. I've spread the melody line over two strings because changing strings is your next hurdle. It's easy enough on a single string after a while, but the act of changing strings can put you right back on the nursery slopes. Take your time, call the fingers out loud and don't allow yourself to get frustrated if you get in a muddle.

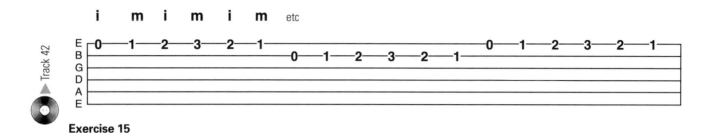

Exercise 15

Exercise 16 brings your right-hand thumb into play. It's quite likely that your thumb will be playing bass lines, chord roots and so on, and a lot of the time these lines move around a bit from string to string. In this exercise, you're playing a scale fragment over three strings in order to get the thumb used to this kind of movement.

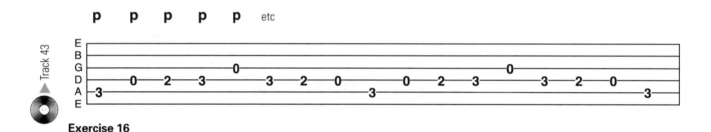

Exercise 16

Exercise 17 is where things become a little more involved, but don't give up. Right-hand independence is what the game of fingerpicking is all about, and this routine will set you on the right path.

We're looking at another scale which is to be played with alternate index and middle fingers. (Notice that I've started you off on the middle finger this time around. Diabolical, ain't I?) The thumb, meanwhile, plays a pedal point in the bass. (Incidentally, *pedal point* is just music speak for a note that repeats under a melody.) Everything is in time and on the beat – I haven't syncopated anything. That would have been cruel. Maybe later, eh?

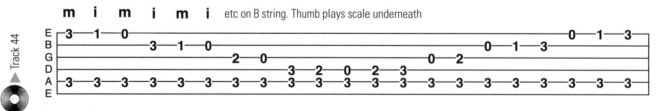

Exercise 17

You'll need to check out the CD and slow things right down for this exercise. Don't give in, though, because we're covering a lot of vital ground.

Exercise 18 twists everything around once again so that the thumb does all the work while the pedal point has moved to the top strings. Look at the fingering on top of the tab closely, though – you might only be playing a single note, but you're still expected to alternate between index and middle fingers.

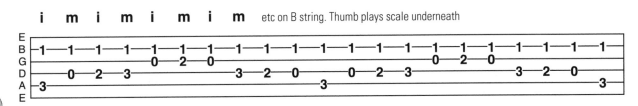

 i m i m i m i m i m m etc on B string. Thumb plays scale underneath

Track 45

Exercise 18

In many ways, these exercises should be included in your practice routine alongside the arpeggios in the little workout we looked at earlier. Together they will do your fingers a lot of good and prepare you well for a great deal of right-hand guitar work. So take care, don't get discouraged if it all seems difficult at first, ignore the "can't do" barrier and avoid all those personal Everests!

Open Strings Are Your Friends

Using open strings in chord voicings can add considerable sparkle to your fingerpicking work in many ways. For one thing, it allows you to overcome one of the shortcomings of the guitar itself, that being standard tuning's resistance to close harmony. If you want a pocket definition of what I mean, consider this: the guitar is tuned in fourths, and this means that notes close to each other in the scale are difficult to put into a single chord shape. For instance, imagine you want to include the semitone C and C# in the same chord shape – difficult, huh? You could use the C at the first fret on the second string, but the nearest C# that's of any use is on the sixth fret, third string – a bit of a stretch. And yet this sort of close harmony can be very effective when used in songs or fingerstyle pieces.

This is where open strings can be a positive boon, and yet you might be thinking that, because there are only six open strings on the guitar, this would be a little limiting. Not so. Well, not really; if you desperately needed to include a certain chord voicing in a chord arrangement and couldn't find it with the open strings at hand, a little experimenting with a capo would probably yield results in 90 per cent of cases. And, of course, the maths necessary to work out exactly where to put the chord and how you were going to rearrange the rest of your piece around the new fret locations would do you no end of good. Trust me.

The other thing that open strings are good for is producing pedal points within pieces. Alter the chord shape but leave the same open string ringing each time and you've called upon a very effective musical device with the minimum of effort. Listen to some of the early work by prog pioneers Genesis for good examples of this technique (especially on pieces like 'Supper's Ready' from their *Foxtrot* album).

Don't worry if some of these definitions sound a bit far-fetched; the exercises we're looking at here should fill in all the blanks for you nicely.

What I want to demonstrate is how easy it is to take advantage of open strings in your arrangements and produce really exotic-sounding chords with no trouble at all. Look at Exercise 19 below. All you have to do is hold down two notes and, just by moving them up a fret in each case, the chord is changed from major to minor at a stroke.

A minor & major chords   **D minor & major chords**   **E minor & major chords**

Track 46

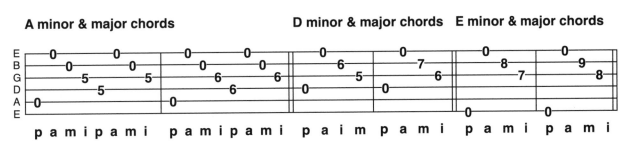

p a m i p a m i   p a m i p a m i   p a i m p a m i   p a m i p a m i

Exercise 19

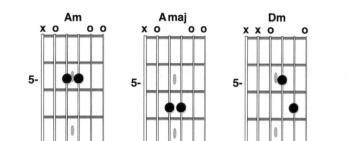
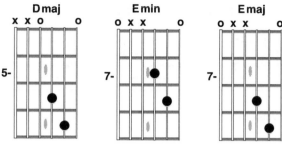

It's pretty effortless stuff and yet so effective at the same time. The fingerpicking patterns aren't anything too new, either; we've looked at similar patterns before.

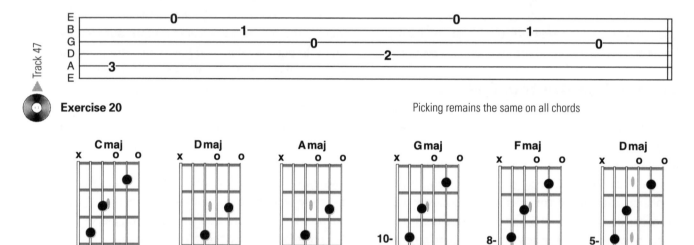

Track 47

Exercise 20

Picking remains the same on all chords

Exercise 20 uses the familiar chord shape of C major and demonstrates how you can move it around the neck and come up with some nice-sounding chords – all from a single shape. Incidentally, when I've named the chords in either the exercise or tab, I've been fairly economical; if I was going to be precise, the voicings contain exotica like ninths and suspended fourths, but I want you to think of them as simply as possible, just major and minor. In this way, they'll be of more use to you.

Exercise 21 uses two basic shapes to navigate the guitar neck, producing some good-sounding chords along the way. You're going to have to make sure that your chord-moving ability is pretty much up to scratch to make this one work, but it's well worth the effort when you practise it up to speed. Songs like Sting's 'Fragile' and 'Bring On The Night' were written using this kind of idea, so you'll be in good company if you can work out some ideas of your own using this example.

Track 48

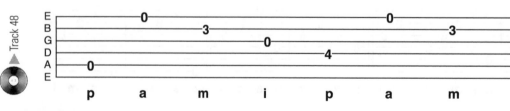

Exercise 21

Picking remains the same throughout the exercise

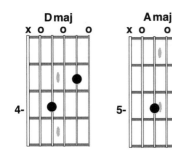
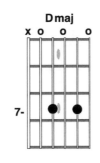
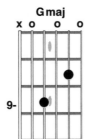
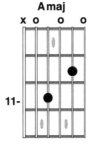
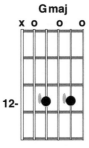

For a couple of these exercises, you might need to practise the right-hand fingerpicking on one of the chords before you start moving anything around. This way, you'll be limiting the number of things you have to look at simultaneously. Remember, as always, to start things off at an easy, moderately slow pace, bringing things slowly up to speed as your confidence increases with each exercise. When everything is flowing freely, try using other fingerpicking patterns on the chords to see what ideas of your own you can come up with.

In general, it's always worth seeing what open strings will do to a chord. Even if you're playing up the neck, beyond the basic "open position" area, a moment or two spent experimenting with some open strings might uncover a chord voicing that appeals to you and will give your guitar playing that extra edge.

Graduation Piece

If you sneaked a look at the section on playing with a pick, you'll have noted how I put a piece at the end of the chapter that took the form of a sort of graduation piece. You'll have read how I tend to believe in 200-year-old solutions to modern-day problems, as most of the areas of technique in both left and right hands

were being addressed way back then and, what's more, no one's really come along with any better ideas since, so if the 200-year-old techniques have existed this long, they probably still have something going for them.

In this instance, we're going to look at an excerpt from a piece by Mauro Giuliani (1781-1829), which happens to be a piece from the student repertoire for classical guitar but sounds like a piece of folky fingerpicking at the same time. (As a footnote, it was also the theme tune to a children's TV show in the UK in around the 1960s called *Tales Of The Riverbank*, and so it might have some built-in nostalgia value for some of you, too.) It's a piece that calls for a lot of the techniques we've been looking at in both right and left hands, although it's probably a lot more kind to the left in that it stays pretty much down at the nut and doesn't call for any stratospheric leaps up the fretboard. This is all well and good, of course, because it allows you to concentrate on what the right hand is getting up to.

It's a good exercise for bringing out the melody line, too, if this is at all a problem area in your playing. Remember, there's no particular trick to this at all; it's just a question of playing the melody notes with slightly more pressure on the string with the right-hand fingers.

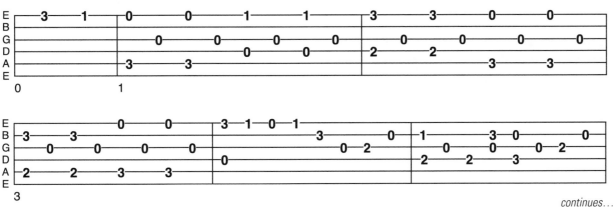

continues…

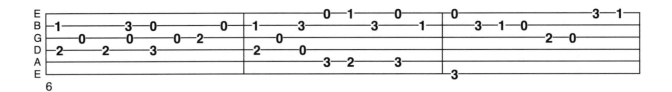

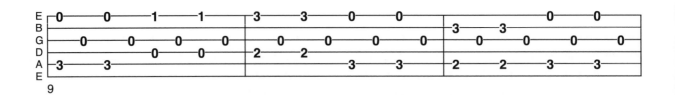

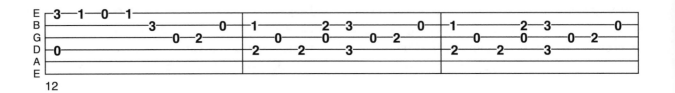

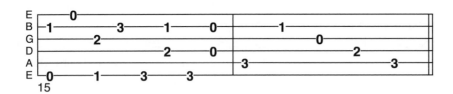

I'll round off this chapter with the most original reason I've ever been given in an interview for someone changing from using a pick to using fingers – in Teddy Royal's case, his thumb.

"I was playing at this club in Chicago called the Other Place and one night it was really, really packed. When we took a break, I was walking offstage and all of a sudden the organist in the band called me to ask me a question. When I turned back, this old man was standing in front of me. He'd appeared from nowhere. He was dressed in black and his hair was grey – he had to be 70 or 80 years old. Anyway, he grabbed my hand and looked me in the eye and said, 'Son, why don't you put the pick down?' The organist called to me again and I turned to him to speak, but when I turned back the old man had vanished. I felt that a spirit had visited me."
Teddy Royal

LEFT-HAND DEVELOPMENT

"The song, to me, dictates the way you treat it."
Mark Knopfler

Whereas the right hand's task really begins and ends with the mechanical aspect of sounding the strings, the left hand's principal task is that of fretboard orientation. To put it another way, it has to know its way about the place really well or some of the guitar's great potential as a music-making machine will never be fully unlocked.

There's muscular development here, too, of course. If you can remember struggling with your first barre chord or even playing an open-position F-major chord for the first time, you'll know all about the physical hurdles that the instrument can throw in your way. But the necessary physical adeptness isn't beyond anyone; you just have to remind yourself that any such development will take time and that it won't come by itself. The quickest route to building up the left hand to become a fully fit member of your guitar-playing team is via patient, persistent practice.

I've had plenty of pupils who've told me they've had a particular problem with a certain aspect of playing, and all have agreed that they've never really addressed the problem with any specific practice routine, believing instead that the problem would eventually go away if they kept playing long enough. In general, I've never found this to be true. Problems remain problems until they're looked at and some device or other has been implemented to sort things out.

So, having said all that, how are we going to start working with the left hand?

Orienteering

I'm absolutely serious when I say that I think the most important task the left hand has is that of knowing its way around. The good thing is that, this being not so much a question of physical challenge, you can do an awful lot of the necessary work away from the guitar.

For a start, I recommend that everyone has a neck chart that shows the locations of all the notes from the open strings up to the twelfth fret. I suggested this when we were looking at chords a few chapters ago, and if you didn't do it then, now's the time. If you want your neck chart to remain uncluttered, don't bother filling in all the sharps and flats; just go for the "whole notes" – A B C D E F G. Then, all you have to remember is that A♭ is one fret lower than A and G♯ is one fret higher than G and so on. This means that your chart remains readable and doesn't look half as foreboding as it would if it had every single note scrawled upon it.

Once your neck chart is complete, you'll be using it to locate barre-chord shapes, scale roots and so on as you map out some of the things we've already taken a look at in this book.

As far as actual physical development is concerned, you can do no better than to initiate a little practice routine that you repeat daily and that comprises some simple stretching exercises and a few scales. Don't go mad – you need only a few minutes a day to warm things up and ensure that things continue to proceed nicely. Physical development will continue as you continue to play. You just need that initial period at the beginning of your practice routine where you challenge yourself a little.

As far as stretching exercises are concerned,

here's one I've been recommending for years. It features in my book *Guitar Workout* (or *Ten Minute Guitar Workout* in the US) and is one that I personally discovered way back in the '70s.

Track 51

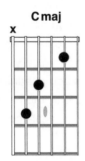
i

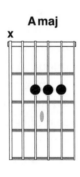
ii

iii

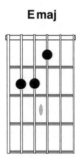
iv

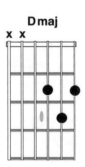
v

Here's what you do. The first shape is "home", and it is from this shape that you play every other. (Initially, you'll be playing from the first shape to the second shape and back again. The next step is to play shapes one, two, one, three, then one. Then one, two, one, three, one, four, one, etc. Get the idea? If not, it's on the CD!) All that's happening with this exercise is that you're swapping the positions of two fingers at once while the others remain in place – and it's harder than it looks. But a couple of minutes doing this exercise feels like the equivalent of 30 minutes in the gym and it's doing your left hand a lot of good. It's an exercise that you can continue to use, too, as a warm-up exercise before a gig or just before practising. Once you've got it sorted out in the fifth position, move your hand down a couple of frets to make the stretch bigger once again.

Cautionary Tale

As with every exercise programme, take very good care not to overdo things. Too much at once will open the door to repetitive-strain problems, so if there's even a whiff of discomfort in your hands, arms, back or anywhere, stop playing and rest for a while. If the problem continues, take a good long look at your playing position, ensuring that your wrists are as straight as possible, that there's no unwanted tension present in your hands or arms and that you're sitting (or standing) in a comfortable position. If things still don't get any better, seek advice from a doctor who specialises in such matters. Whatever you do, take care while you're in the "development" stages of playing as any damage you inflict now by adopting bad habits will take a long time to put right.

Mapping Out The Fretboard

I'm taking for granted that you've already familiarised yourself with the simple chords down at the guitar's nut. We often refer to these chords as being *open position* or *first position*, and basically they comprise chords like these:

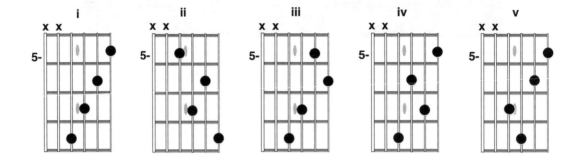
C maj   A maj   G maj   E maj   D maj

You may have come across barre chords like these, too:

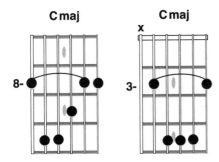

If not, learning to cope with barre chords should definitely be your next step. Just taking the shapes above and using your neck chart to find major-chord positions all over the fretboard will start the orientating process off nicely, but in order to do the job thoroughly you'll need a bit more of a system, and there is a very good one that has been around since the '60s. It's called the CAGED system, and this is how it works.

If you've explored the various barre-chord shapes available on the fretboard, you'll have noticed that there are quite a few different ways of playing each chord, but we can extend and systemise this to our advantage. Let's look at how the chord of C major repeats up the fretboard.

First of all, here's the shape that everyone comes across for C major quite early on:

If you've already read the chapter on chords, you'll now know that this shape is made up exclusively of

the notes C, E and G. The next time we find a convenient location for the chord of C major, it's here at the third fret:

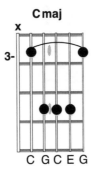

If we were going to give this particular shape a name, we'd probably opt for calling it an "A-shape barre chord" because of its resemblance to the open position for A down at the nut. Musically, it comprises the notes C, E and G, once again, and so its full (colloquial) title would probably be "an A-shape C-major chord" or something like that. (Don't confuse the term "shape" with the musical name of the chord.)

The next familiar face we find in the guise of C major looks like this:

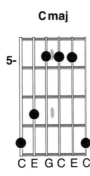

It looks like a G-shape chord, and it's a bit of a monster to play as a fully functioning barre chord, but don't worry too much about that for now. It's the location of the chord that we're more concerned about in this instance.

At around the eighth fret, we hit something you'll probably be familiar with already:

Cmaj

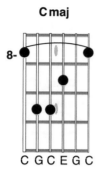

C G C E G C

It looks like an open-position E chord, but it's made up once again from the notes C, E and G, which puts the firm stamp of C major upon it. Naturally, this is known as an "E-shape barre chord".

There's one more version of C major to consider before we hit the twelfth fret and everything starts to repeat. This time, it's a D-shape chord, but the notes it contains identifies it as C major.

Cmaj

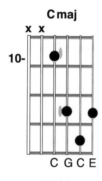

C G C E

If we proceed any further, we find this:

Cmaj

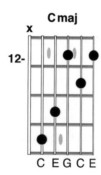

C E G C E

Definitely a C chord this time, and in the same

relative position as the open-position version, twelve frets lower. In practical terms, this chord and anything above it is probably worth considering only from a practical point of view if you have a cutaway acoustic, allowing easier access to the higher fret positions.

So what exactly have we got here? We've seen that a single chord – in this case C major – repeats up the guitar fretboard like this: open C shape, barre A shape, barre G shape, barre E shape and D shape. Put it together and you spell out the word *CAGED*. This isn't too difficult to remember and forms the beginnings of a fretboard system that will unlock many of the guitar's secrets for you. One of the principal reasons why this trick is so useful is, of course, that it works in any key.

Let's look at another key and apply the CAGED system to it. We'll pick G.

Gmaj

The first chord shape for G we encounter is the well-known open shape around the third fret. So what's next? If you said E then whoop for joy because you're spot on. If you're just pretending that you knew the answer all along, consider this: caGEd – E follows G in the word *CAGED*. It really is as simple as that. Here it is:

Gmaj

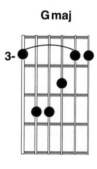

If we think along the lines of cagED, we'll probably all agree that the next in line for the G-chord round-up is the D shape, shown here:

G maj

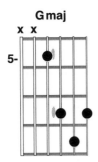

If we've reached the D version for G major, there's only one place to go now and that's back to the beginning of the word *CAGED* and look for a C shape.

G maj

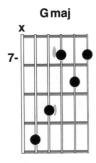

And finally, the A shape clocks in at around the tenth fret:

G maj

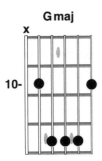

Once again, all of the different versions spell out *CAGED* on the fretboard (well, in this case they spell out GEDCA, but you know what I mean). The key to finding the exact location of major chords using this

system is knowing where the various root notes are in the five basic chord shapes involved, and here they are:

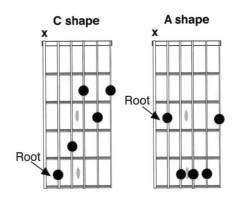

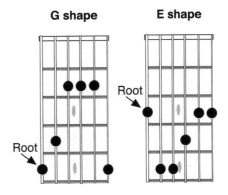

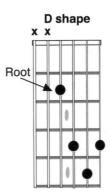

If you look at your neck chart in relation to the work we've done in the two keys we've already covered, you'll see that all of the Cs are where they should be in the C version of the CAGED procession and all the Gs are in their places when we swap over to the key of G.

To explore the CAGED system more fully, spend a little time finding out where the various chords fall in other keys. Remember, it's always going to spell CAGED, even if it starts halfway through the word. It might help if you think of it like this:

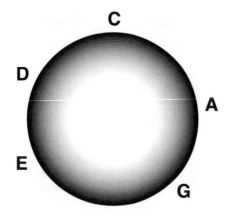

Chords progress up the neck in a clockwise direction and down the neck anticlockwise

Then, at whatever point you choose to hop onto the circle, you'll know what you're going to encounter next.

Overview

Without a doubt, the CAGED system is a seriously useful tool when it comes to fretboard orienteering. I learned it from the great jazz player Joe Pass way back in 1981 and it completely revolutionised my ideas about the fretboard.

If you extend the system one stage further and start linking chord shapes to scale shapes, you're entering into very serious territory indeed. Remember those scale shapes for C major that we looked at back in the "Painless Music Theory" chapters on chords and scales? Well, here they are again, with their corresponding chord shapes outlined inside.

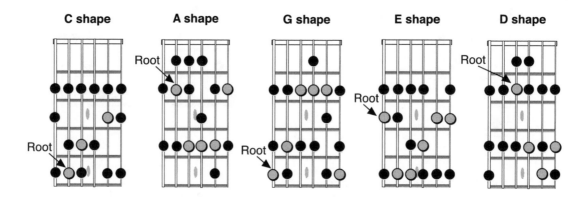

| C shape | A shape | G shape | E shape | D shape |

Now you can see more of the CAGED system's full potential, because those scale shapes are always going to link up with the chords they contain in every key, and so you've amassed an awful lot of information all at once. It's probably a good idea to write down the scales in a couple of different keys just to ram the idea well and truly home. Eventually, it will become like very simple mental arithmetic, and after that you won't even need a system because you'll begin to know where everything is instinctively.

Left-Hand Technique

Apart from changing between chord shapes with the agility of a mountain goat and playing seamless

melodic passages effortlessly, there are a few specific techniques worth looking at when it comes to considering the left hand's role in guitar playing. (Incidentally, if you're left handed and have decided to play the guitar in a "mirrored" playing position to the right handers, the tips in these chapters on left- and right-hand assignments are going to need reversing.)

The most important playing technique that the left hand can apply is that of vibrato. If you deconstruct any given player's technique, hoping to find out just what it is that makes it so individual, you'll find that vibrato is particularly important. A lot of the time, vibrato is very much a player's individual musical thumbprint, as it plays a very large part in the actual shaping of each note.

Rock guitarists playing on light-gauge strings can really make the most of this technique, and arguably it's the rock arena in which more variations exist. But when you consider that vibrato comes into play in classical guitar and that its presence there is every bit as vital a tonal tool, it's easy to understand why we're going to spend time considering the technique here.

Basically, there are two different types of vibrato: one is more common to classical guitar – and most classical instruments, for that matter – and as such is also known as *violin vibrato*, while the other is more associated with blues and rock guitar. The two types differ mainly in the fact that the classical variant has the left-hand finger moving from side to side horizontally along the string whereas blues vibrato calls for the finger to move from side to side vertically. In general, the latter form of vibrato is more effective on steel-string guitar, with the classical vibrato being far more subtle, but it's certainly worth familiarising yourself with both types so that you can choose either style for yourself to fit any given playing circumstance. There are demonstrations of both types of vibrato on the accompanying CD, if you're still in doubt.

Classical Vibrato

Track 52

Hold your guitar in the normal playing position so that the neck is roughly horizontal to the floor and then fret a note and roll your finger from left to right along the string's length. Be sure not to make big movements with the fingertip and keep the finger on the string at all times. Essentially, the point of the fingertip doesn't travel along the string; the movement depends more on the flexibility of the fingertip itself.

The effect produced with classical vibrato offers only the slightest contour to the note but it has the effect, to my ears, of sweetening things up considerably. It's not a technique that necessarily comes naturally to an awful lot of players, however, so be prepared to persevere for a while before things start sounding absolutely right.

Blues Vibrato

Track 53

Blues vibrato differs from the classical variety in that it's far more pronounced and, some would say, more dramatic. For this style of vibrato, the finger moves up and down in relation to the guitar neck's horizontal relationship to the floor. On the fretboard, this means that you're alternately pulling and pushing the string out of position, which is why the effect is more pronounced – you're literally changing the pitch of the string far more than a simple along-the-string motion possibly could.

This technique also calls for much more control before it starts to sound good, as the push-and-pull factor has to be about equal before it works. In other words, a lot of players who are new to this technique find that their vibrato sounds uneven or out of tune because they aren't moving the string evenly enough.

Once again, good vibrato calls for systematic practice – don't leave it aside in the hope that it will develop by itself. Spend a little time during your practice routine polishing it up, as it's a vitally important tool to have at hand.

If I needed to push home the message of how important vibrato is as a tonal medium still further, I'd go as far as to say that, whenever students complain to me at seminars or in lessons that their sound is still very untogether, I look at their vibrato technique first and generally find that this is the seat of their problems.

String Bending

This is a technique that really is more in the domain of the rock and blues player, but a more subtle, refined and occasional variation crops up on acoustic guitar, so it's worth mentioning.

Your worst enemy here is the fact that you will have far heavier strings on your acoustic guitar than you probably would have on an electric. I know of only one player who has the same gauge on his electric and acoustic guitar. Most of us opt for lightish strings on electric and medium-to-heavy gauge on acoustic. This gives both types of instrument a very specific feel, under normal circumstances, and it's maybe easier to understand that there's one set of rules for acoustic and another set of contrasting rules for electric. So it's probably not hard to understand that a .012 string is going to be more of a challenge to bend than a .009 – and we're only talking top strings here. The other thing to consider is that the third string on an acoustic guitar is wound, making it less flexible in the bending department to quite a considerable degree.

Given that the job at hand has its drawbacks when compared to bending strings on an electric, the actual technique is almost exactly the same. I'd suggest that you start your bending experiments on your second string, the B. Try playing a note around halfway up the fretboard – say, around the seventh fret – with your third finger. Place fingers one and two behind your third and use them to help you push the string away from its pitch. If you want to know how far to bend the string, try playing fret eight first, remember the pitch and try to push the string at fret seven to the same note.

Musically, what's happening is that you're bending the pitch of the note from F♯ to G, a semitone's distance. Play both notes a few times to give your brain time to appreciate the points of departure and arrival. Time and practice will see to it that you become more and more accurate in your bending endeavours.

Bending on the other strings calls for slight variations in the basic technique. For instance, when you get over to the lower strings, a lot of players prefer to pull the strings down towards the floor rather than push them upwards. Of course, on the bass string, you've got no choice, as pushing would cause the string to come off the side of the neck. Similarly, you couldn't expect to pull the top E string, for the same reason.

Sliding

Track 54

Most of the time, when you change frets while playing a melody or a scale, you use two separate fingers to do so and you most likely pluck twice, too. Sliding is a technique whereby you pluck the note once and slide the finger along the string to another pitch. In this respect, it's an alternative to bending – it's easier on the fingers, too – but the effect it produces is almost entirely different.

To experiment with sliding, play the seventh fret on the G string (D) and slide to the ninth fret (E) just after you pick it. The effect produced should be a smooth change of pitch.

Many people, when they try this for the first time, do one of two things: they either forget to stop or they look at me with pain in their eyes and say, "Ouch!" You're probably already aware of the somewhat calamitous amount of wear and tear on the fingertips produced by guitar playing, and sliding is a case in point. Stop whining. It's worth it.

At its most basic, this technique might not sound worth the effort, but taken a little further down the line it becomes a very useful tool and you'll find it cropping up quite a lot. For instance, moving between scale shapes will necessitate some sliding, and so, once again, some time spent digging the foundations here will ensure a smoother transition to the fully fledged version of the technique later on.

All you have to do is practise sliding from one pitch to another along a single string until everything begins to sound smooth and tuneful.

Slurs

There are two techniques nestling under this particular banner, colloquially known as "hammer-ons" and "pull-offs". In a functional sense, both add up to being slurs, which effectively means that you play more than one note from a single pluck or pick of the guitar string. There are electric-guitar players who use slurring to a great extent and their style is said to be *legato*, which means "smooth" or "flowing". This is (arguably) easier to do on electric guitar using a fair amount of gain on the amplifier, which has the effect of making everything touch-sensitive. Acoustic guitarists don't benefit from the same set of advantages, but the technique still crops up very often within any melodic style.

Hammer-Ons

Track 55

The hammer-on is a technique whereby you would pick a fretted note and literally hammer down one or more fingers from the left hand, which has the effect of actually sounding the notes involved.

As an example, place your first finger on, say, the fifth fret of the G string, pluck the note with the right hand (or plectrum or whatever) and then immediately hammer down the third finger on the seventh fret.

Hammer-On

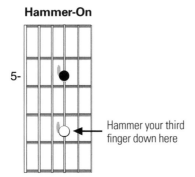

5-

← Hammer your third finger down here

Pull-Off

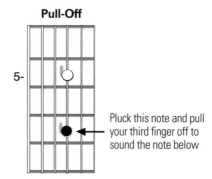

5-

← Pluck this note and pull your third finger off to sound the note below

There are a couple of examples on the CD, if you're not sure what this technique should sound like. The main thing to make sure of here is that both notes are approximately the same volume; the only thing missing from a sonic perspective should be the pluck before the second note.

You can hear the difference between a plucked and hammered note by repeating the above exercise, but this time picking both notes. The slurred version should sound smooth, whereas the picked version will sound like two separate events. As I say, listen to the CD if you're at all unsure.

Extending this technique further would involve playing a scale passage, picking each string only once.

Hammer-On Scale

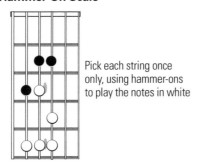

Pick each string once only, using hammer-ons to play the notes in white

Once again, the effect here is smooth and slightly less defined than it would be if the notes were each plucked separately.

Pull-Offs

Track 56

The exact opposite of a hammer-on is a pull-off. We can repeat the experiment we tried above, but this time it's reversed so that we start with the note at the seventh fret on the G string.

Note that the first finger is in place, ready and waiting, because once you've sounded the note at the seventh fret, you immediately lift the third finger off, which should have the effect of sounding the note at the fifth. You might find that you have to drag the tip of the third finger very slightly across the string, as opposed to merely lifting it vertically, which will help put some movement into the string. Listen to the CD for an aural demonstration.

If we extend this idea into everyday playing, it's once again possible to sound a whole series of notes in this way (along a single string, obviously). Try this:

Multiple Pull-Offs

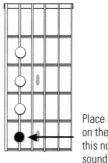

← Place all four fingers on the string and pluck this note, pulling off to sound the others

Play the note being held down by the little finger and carefully drag the fingers off one at a time until you reach the first finger. The effect should sound like a smooth transition from note to note.

Combining The Two

When your hammer and pull technology is well up to speed, another technique becomes available to you: the trill. The word *trill* is actually very old fashioned, as it belongs to the set of ornaments that have been employed in lute and classical guitar since the

Track 57

Renaissance. It's just one of those words that contemporary music has never got around to replacing. In effect, a trill is a repetitive series of hammers and pulls. The series could be short or long, according to what's called for in the music, but the basic technique remains pretty much the same.

If we play the two notes at the fifth and seventh frets on the G string, once again, first strike the note at the fifth fret, immediately hammer on the seventh and then instantly remove it. Repeat as often as necessary. Again, I've put down a few aural clues on the CD in case you have trouble imagining what the technique should sound like.

In practice, it's not the norm to pick every single note you play, and hammers, pulls and trills help you bring about this economy. If everything were picked, it would have a dynamic effect like that of a machine gun – every note you played would have that distinctive *plick* noise at the beginning and fast passages, especially, would sound fragmented. Employing a healthy dose of slurring technique in your melody lines ensures that everything sounds flowing and musical.

Thumbs Up

When I started playing, back in guitar's Dark Ages, the major controversy was whether or not you should use your left-hand little finger. The little finger received an awful lot of bad press in the early days, as it was considered very much the runt of the litter on both hands. Many players were of the opinion that this smallest of digits was far too weak to be of any real use and opted instead to use the three main fingers of the left hand exclusively. Today, even the right-hand little finger comes in for occasional use in some classical pieces and use of its left-hand equivalent is commonplace.

A finger that also gets called into service every so often now is the left-hand thumb – and the debate is over; it's already in use in many pieces. Under normal circumstances, the natural playing position for the left hand calls for the thumb to be extended a little over the upper side of the guitar neck, so it's not really stretching things too far to expect it to be called into use every so often when the odd sixth-string bass note is called for and it's the only finger free.

An example of an occasion when the thumb is called into action is shown below:

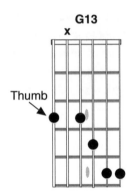

Of course, it's not necessary to finger the chord above using your thumb on the bass string; this is only an example. This action might feel a little strange at first, as it clenches the fist a little, putting more tension into the hand, but just tell yourself that you'll be doing this kind of thing only quite rarely and certainly not in day-to-day playing.

Summing Up

Remember that one of the most characteristic things about a guitarist is his sound, and both hands can play a dramatic role in producing this all-important sonic signature. All of the techniques listed above are worthy of your attention and will add to your own personal tonal palette as you interpret and use them in your own way.

USING A CAPO

"A capo is an amazing thing."
Mark Knopfler

Just about every acoustic guitarist in the popular domain has used a capo at one time or another. Watch any performance video by Paul Simon, Mark Knopfler or James Taylor, for example, and you'll spot one of these little mechanical devices clamped to the guitar neck at some point in the proceedings. But have you ever asked yourself why, exactly? I mean, don't these guys know how to transpose their songs into different keys yet? Have they not mastered barre chords, or what? Seriously, the capo probably receives a lot of bad press for being a crutch for a lack of knowledge or a technical cop-out, although that couldn't be further from the truth.

Far from being some sort of synthetic additive to give a guitar player something with which to prop up his crumbling technique, a capo is actually a seriously creative little device that can enhance your ability and set your creative juices flowing.

The Controversial Bit

We stirred up a storm in *Guitar Techniques* magazine many times in the past because of the way we transcribed pieces where a capo has been employed. The *GT* method is to notate the position of your capo on the guitar neck as "0", because the capo takes over from the nut and generates its own open strings. Convention, on the other hand, would have it that wherever you strap on your capo remains a numbered position. For instance, if you were to put a capo on at the fifth fret, the "open" strings created by this action would show up in the tab as "5" all the time. We would transcribe it as "0" and stubbornly refuse to believe that our way isn't the easier-to-understand method.

Instinctively, a guitarist seeing "5" in tab would be inclined to try to fret it, forgetting the fact that the capo's doing all the work for him, but when the average guitarist sees "0" in tab notation he intuitively employs an open string at that point, irrespective of whether a capo is there or not. Worse still, the conventional way around will sometimes employ an even more diabolical system whereby the capo position is indeed numbered "0" but whichever fret is next in line to the capo position is numbered "1", no matter where it lies on the neck. So, in our hypothetical scenario where we have a capo on the fifth fret, the sixth would be labelled as "1". Confused? We were, and so this is why hours of debate led us to formulating the system we now use. So, to recap, the actual capo fret is always going to be "0" and nothing else changes.

I'm glad we sorted that out. Now all we've got to do is oil the flap on my letterbox and wait for the outcry from the acoustic fraternity that I'm a heretic.

Capos In General

Capos come in all different shapes and sizes, ranging from the very cheap metal bar on a piece of elastic right up to the more sophisticated mechanical wonder that slips on and off the guitar neck with no fuss at all. The best news is that, even at the Rolls-Royce end of things, capos still sell for a relatively modest £15 or so. Go on, spoil yourself.

Use And Abuse

"I think [a capo] can add so much variety. The ear gets used to hearing normal open-position

chords like D, G and A minor or whatever, and just having a capo on the second or third fret can make it sound that little bit more unusual."
Marillion's Steve Rothery

Way back when I was learning guitar (when beer tasted better and the summers were longer, etc), the humble capo enjoyed a somewhat dubious reputation as being strictly a folk thing. And, of course, they carried with them all the jibes mentioned above, about their owners not being able to do barre chords. What this added up to was an almost subterranean usage by rock players. And you never, ever saw an electric guitarist using one, no siree. Unless you saw Albert Collins live, of course.

Then, gradually, things began to fall into place. You'd go and buy a Simon And Garfunkel songbook and find out that there were songs in there that were totally unplayable because they were in all the hard keys, like E flat, and why would Paul Simon go and do something mad like write in a totally awkward key like that? The answer was in two parts: the first was all about finding a key that suited both Paul Simon and Art Garfunkel's very different vocal ranges, and the second was that Simon was using a capo. *Click!* Everything fell into place. What's more, if it was OK for Paul Simon, then maybe the rest of us could take capos altogether more seriously. At last, the capo came out of the closet, got respectable and settled down to a relatively normal life.

The revelations didn't stop in my formative years, either. I interviewed Mark Knopfler once and mentioned that, during my guitar-teaching days, his song 'Romeo And Juliet' came up with alarming frequency. I went on to say that it had always given me a problem, in terms of coming up with a set of fingering for it that worked. Before I got to the end of my sentence, though, Mark said, "It's a G tuning with a capo on the third fret." D'oh.

"'Down Down', that's a G tuning with a capo on the fourth fret, and 'Mystery Song' is a G tuning [which] brings you into the key of A. Rick loves his tunings. I don't know why." *Francis Rossi*

Avoiding The Mental Arithmetic
Imagine a songwriter coming up with a nice set of chords down at the nut of his guitar. Some of them might use open strings, perhaps, and so any attempt at transposing the idea using barre chords would make life very difficult. But hang on – just strapping on a capo and trying it at various frets would inevitably result in him finding a spot where the key is right for his (or the intended singer's) voice. To him, he would still be playing an open G with a nice-sounding little F♯ stuck in the middle to give a major-seventh sound, but having a capo on the third fret would mean that he was, in fact, playing the chord B♭ maj7.

The important thing here is that he probably wouldn't care; it's merely a means to an end and, if necessary, all the science can be worked out later, if anything needs to be written down and passed on to other band members. So don't tie yourself in a knot worrying about what a chord arrangement actually becomes in terms of chord names or key when you use a capo. Explore all of the new timbres available to you in this way and leave the worrying until later.

Back To The Plot
What I'm going to do is try to introduce you to how the capo can be used as a creative tool for your acoustic pursuits, irrespective of whether you're a singer/songwriter or the new Michael Hedges. (Incidentally, all you really have to learn for this particular lesson is how to listen. Sounds easy? Well, it is. In a way.)

What I've done on the CD is to record the same fingerpicking pattern three times: once on open strings, once with the capo at the fifth fret and once with it at the seventh. What I'd like you to do is to play all of the examples yourself and listen to how playing exactly the same thing at three different pitches offers up an alternate timbre each time. We're talking texture here. Sometimes, you can have an idea for a song or a series of chords that sounds fine when played down at the nut but springs into an entirely different and far more boisterous existence when played again around the fourth fret using a capo.

The actual fingerpicking pattern I've set up is fairly easy, and so it shouldn't make listening to yourself too difficult. Experiment around the chords and see what variations you can come up with. I think you'll be surprised at the difference such a relatively cheap addition to your guitar-playing gear can make.

Open Position

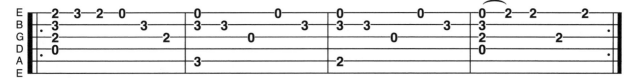

Capo At Fifth Fret

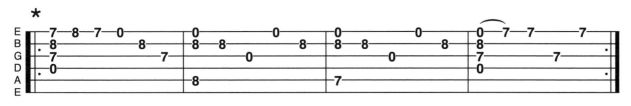

Capo At Seventh Fret

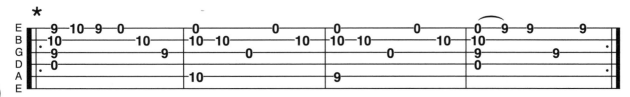

* Remember that the "0" represents the position of the capo

The Mental Arithmetic

Normally, I'd say that you could skip this paragraph if you didn't want to use a capo from a purely tactical point of view – that is, how to use it in such a way that it can provide the answer to questions like "How can I play chords I know but end up playing in A flat?". But, seeing as I really think you ought to read it anyway, I'll try to include a few secrets of the universe along the way.

If you want to use a capo strategically, you need to know a couple of things. First off, you need to know where the root notes are in all the familiar nut-position chords. I've included a few examples below – it's not an exhaustive selection, but it should serve to give you the right idea.

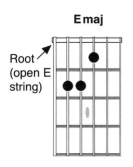
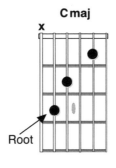
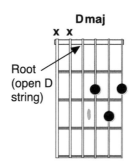
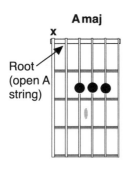
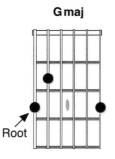

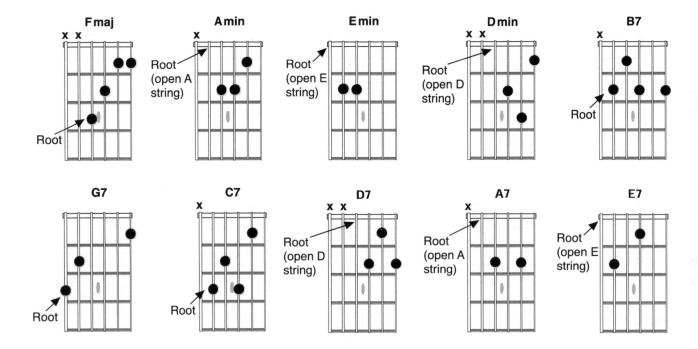

The next thing you need is a chart that shows you where all the notes are on the neck. (I recommended a few chapters ago that you should make yourself a chart like this and so, if you did, you'll be steps ahead. If not, imagine I'm pulling a grumpy face until you slope off and fetch your crayons.)

Now you need to be able to put the two elements together to form a cohesive whole. This is almost exactly the same process that you use to start orienteering with barre chords on the fingerboard. You know when you have an "E-shape" barre chord like this one:

All you have to do is match the note on the sixth string with any other pitch along it and you end up with a major chord of that name. Now, that sounds too much like a rule in a science book, and so here's a more brain-friendly way of getting the same info across without the migraine.

Here's your E-shape barre chord at the third fret. The note on the sixth string (highlighted here for your convenience) is a G, and so the chord is called G major.

G maj

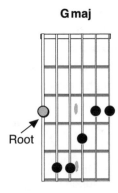

Here's the same shape chord at the eighth fret, lined up with the note C, and so the resulting chord is called C major.

C maj

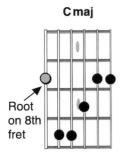

Root on 8th fret

This time, the root notes line up with the note F♯, making this an F♯ major chord. While we're here, if we try playing a few other root-position chords, let's see what we get.

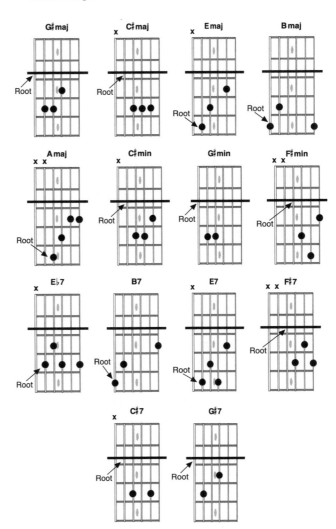

Capo At 4th Fret

If I know my reader correctly, I think you probably got the idea way back when I introduced the original concept a couple of paragraphs ago. The illustrations are really here just to make the page look pretty.

OK, so are we all agreed now that this particular way of doing things is fairly simple to get to grips with? Well, in that case, let's take a couple of chord shapes that aren't particularly barre-friendly and let the capo do all of the hard work instead of our poor index fingers.

Here's a D-major chord, down at the nut, in what we guitar teachers call "root position".

D maj

x x

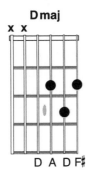

D A D F♯

As you can see, there are two Ds present in this chord shape, and we can use either of them to move the chord around using a capo in order to come up with another chord in a different key. Say that we strap the capo on at the fourth fret and play the same shape again, like this:

F♯ maj

Capo at the fourth fret

Can you see what's happening here? A little bit of fairly simple mental arithmetic gives us access to a whole range of "awkward" chords while using only chords that have been with us all along the way.

More Good News

Of course, you're not going to be using a capo for single chords or even strapping it on in the middle of a song or piece. (Interestingly enough, I've seen James Taylor change the position of his capo mid-song to facilitate a key change – see "The Quirk Factor" in the

"Introduction".) The good news here is that, because of the very science of music and the way in which chord arrangements tend to group chords in predictable huddles, a capo is even more useful to you than in the ways I've described so far.

To illustrate this, let's take a perfectly straightforward-looking chord arrangement down at the nut:

|| A / / / | D / / / | E / / / | A / / / |
| F♯min / / / | B min / / / | A / / / ||

And here below are the shapes you'd be almost sure to use. It involves a couple of barres along the way, but that's par for the course. (We're not going to be using the capo as a crutch for poor barre technique, remember?)

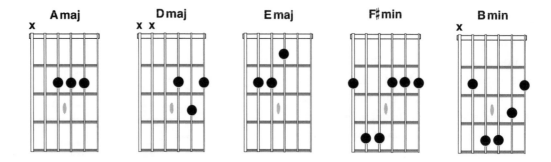

Here's what the same chord arrangement would look like in a different key:

|| D♭ / / / | F♯ / / / | A♭ / / / | D♭ / / / |
| B♭min / / / | E♭ min / / / | D♭ / / / ||

Looks absolutely horrifying, doesn't it? Sure, we could use barre chords pretty much all the way through, but

if we want to maintain the uniformity of the nut-based original we've just got to decide exactly where we're going to strap on the capo. If you refer back to the neck chart I gave you a few paragraphs ago, you'll see that D♭, A♭ and F♯ all fall at the fourth fret, and that gives us the principal clue about where to look for a capo position. Indeed, employing the capo at the fourth fret would give us this:

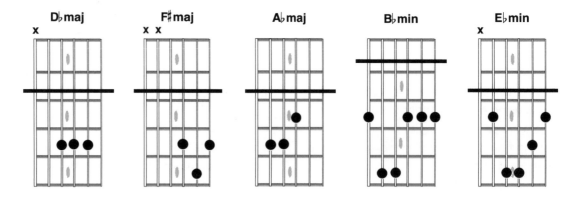

Look familiar? The chances are that any song you come across the music for that seems to have been written in an extremely awkward key will mean that, on the original version, the performer used a capo. It's not a

hard-and-fast rule, of course; there is a possibility that the guitarist concerned was using a tuning, in which case I direct you to the chapter on "Altered Tunings" in order to fulfil your new-found role as guitar detective.

WALKING THE STYLE MILE

"When it comes to teaching, I'm all in favour of understanding and learning certain factual things to do with style, but I think beyond that you'd be better off to take as a model either jazz or folk music and try to play with the idiom or style but let the interpretation be totally personal." John Williams

I guess that we're all drawn to particular styles pretty much from day one, as far as playing is concerned, and yet, realistically speaking, style is really only the icing on the cake in terms of actually learning to play. If you wanted to play acoustic blues or jazz, many of the fundamentals are exactly the same, technique-wise; it's just the final few layers that identify what you're up to.

Having said that, of course, as a teacher I find that many people come to me asking for advice about how they should make their initial inroads into playing any given particular style. After years of thought, I came up with the idea that adopting a style is down to three things: repertoire, vocabulary and technique.

Repertoire

Let's consider the differences between rock, blues and jazz as an illustration of how this system works. I believe that the place to begin exploring any style is in the repertoire it draws from. If your interest is in blues, for instance, a good first step would be to seek out some recordings of acoustic blues from different eras and take a listen to what's on offer. Then, once you've established an area in which you think you'd like to work, look at the songs themselves and, if need be, look for the music or, better still, work out some of the songs. This will provide you with some very important information at a basic level. Quite often, the actual sound of a style is inherent in the repertoire it draws from and so you're at least part of the way there, yet you've changed or adapted nothing.

This is particularly relevant when it comes to jazz. One of the principal reasons why jazz sounds the way it does is because of the material it uses at its core. If you've heard a jazz musician muttering that they don't write songs the way they used to, in jazz terms nothing could be closer to the truth. Song structures from the "standard songbook" are very different to the way songs are written these days, which is why there are so few (ie hardly any) new songs that lend themselves to jazz treatment.

And yet jazz was the pop music of its day. The fact that an average song might have a long intro, then a refrain and a chorus and wandered through a couple of key changes before it returned to the main melody was the acceptable standard. Just playing through pieces like 'I Got Rhythm' or 'Stardust' will give anyone a very good idea of the origins of jazz.

The chords employed in the songs were richer in terms of content, too. It was fairly commonplace to have extended dominant sevenths (see "Painless Music Theory I") like 13$\flat$9s or 7$\sharp$5s sitting alongside straight major and minor chords, and that's definitely something you don't see too often today, if at all.

So, as far as jazz is concerned (and more on this in a moment), just the simple act of getting hold of a book of standards and working through them is a very good way of introducing yourself to the style. The same goes for rock acoustic, too. Check out some of the repertoire and you'll very soon become familiar with picking styles, chord voicings, strumming patterns and so on, just by learning some of the tunes.

Vocabulary

If I can draw a few more comparisons between music and language, I'd sum up vocabulary as being the more colloquial aspects of any given style that you would necessarily have to add to your own musical lexicon in order to be fully functional within that style. If we continue to consider blues and jazz here, for blues you would certainly have to explore the full implications of the blues scale in both major and minor keys, become fully conversant with dominant-seventh and ninth chords and look at some of the style's signature mannerisms. For jazz, your scale vocabulary would have to increase to encompass the altered dominant variations (ie what happens when you insert a sharp fifth or other extensions into a dominant scale), and you'd have to know how to use them, too.

Technique

We've seen how different music styles tend to call for you learning new vocabulary. Well, believe it or not, there is such a thing as *colloquial technique*, too. Continuing our brief consideration of the differences in application between blues and jazz in order to highlight what I mean by colloquial technique, let's talk blues for a moment.

I guess the first decision you'd have to make here is whether you were going to be playing fingerstyle or not. If so, there's an area of technique already outlined for you. If you were going to be self-accompanied, you'd have to look at the technique of keeping a solid rhythm going while you sang or played over the top. You might need to look into playing some bass lines under chords, too, and probably learn how to damp chords down at the bridge with the fleshy part of your right hand – things like that.

Jazz, on the other hand, might see you exploring a plectrum style. You might be keen on the Django Reinhardt style of Gypsy jazz, in which case single-note soloing would call for more work with a metronome in the scale-playing department. If you wanted to play chord-melody-style jazz, like Martin Taylor or Joe Pass, you'd have to spend time developing your right-hand technique.

All of this might seem a very cold and clinical approach to adopting a new style, but I believe that, if everything is split into these three main sections, the job is a lot more organised. Let's take a closer look at how you can begin your studies with regard to a couple of the styles mentioned above.

Blues

"The lineage is really like this: my first role model was my dad. I learned his repertoire, and that was everything from spirituals to work songs – basically American folk material from the South. Then it went from my dad to Odetta – she was the next big role model who I emulated. Then it was Richie Havens and then Taj Mahal. Somewhere along the line, this guy called Eric Bibb emerged." *Eric Bibb*

Many players will tell you that, if you can't play blues, you can't play anything. It's one of the fundamentals of the way in which we look at not only the guitar but music itself today. Its origins as a recognisable music form sprang from the Mississippi Delta region of the USA, and the early style of acoustic blues was all summed up in the playing of Robert Johnson. Anyone who is serious about studying the blues should have Johnson's material in their record collections. Effectively, there is only one album to buy (or two if you want all the alternate takes as well), as Johnson's life and career were short.

From there, study all of the pre- and post-war players and discover what each of them brought to the music.

"To be honest, Robert Johnson – which was really 1937-8 – represented the end of the development of the blues. It was the last thing before the whole blues market died because of lack of shellac during the war, and so record manufacturers weren't allowed to do anything. In fact, Robert Johnson is the final refinement of the blues before the whole scene completely changes into moving away out of the blues into other areas.

"You didn't hear any blues recorded until around 1920 with singers like Bessie Smith and Ma Rainey. They picked up the feeling of country blues that they had heard as part of their youth culture, what they heard when they were four or five. So that takes us back to the turn of the century – it's the 1880s, 1890s and 1900s which are the interesting bits, because it's all conjecture and speculation. We can only speculate what kind of music was being played then, but that would have been the original country blues. It certainly wasn't actually in a twelve-bar form as we know it today.

"When it came to the end of 1938 and there was no more Robert Johnson and the war came along, nothing really happened, except guys played what they heard around them. It went back into itself and probably, if one listens to the Muddy Waters *Plantations Recordings* on Chess, which was recorded in 1942, that's probably the state of play where everything has come from since. There was your hiatus point, because after the war electricity was invented – for the guitarist, anyway – and the change in the rhythm I suppose made people think that Robert Johnson was the inventor. But, having said that, I've met people who think that Stevie Ray Vaughan invented the blues!" *King Rollo*

Harmony

"When you first hear it, you think that it sounds fairly simple. But then, when you get actually inside it and try to make those sounds, you find that it's actually impossible! Then you have inspirations and insights – I don't know where they come from, but I was very fortunate in my career to have worked with a lot of these 'rediscovered' artists. From 1962 to '68, I was on shows with Fred McDowell and Bukka White, Son House, Lightnin' Hopkins and John Lee Hooker when they were playing solo acoustic, and when you see something done, you know that it's possible. To hear it on a recording, you think it's impossible. But then you see some of these guys actually doing it." *John Hammond on learning the early blues style*

Unlike jazz, blues harmony isn't really all that complex, relying as it does on dominant sevenths, which are perhaps stretched as far as ninths but generally no further. However, it's a mistake to think that the blues begins and ends with the twelve-bar blues. It's true to say that many blues standards are constructed from a chord arrangement similar to the one shown below, but it's far from the truth to think that it's this chord structure that dominates blues music exclusively.

Twelve-Bar Blues Form

A7 / / /	D7 / / /	A7 / / /	A7 / / /
D7 / / /	D7 / / /	A7 / / /	A7 / / /
E7 / / /	D7 / / /	A7 / / /	A7 / / /

Of course, you'd be forgiven for thinking that the twelve-bar blues is the only available harmonic structure in blues if you attended a jam session. It's common ground for an awful lot of musicians, but it shouldn't represent the full gamut of your exploration into blues, in terms of repertoire. For instance, an awful lot of blues is based on this chord structure:

| A7 / / / | A7 / / / | D7 / / / | D#°7 / / / |
| A7 / F#7 / | B7 / E7 / | A7 / D7 / | A7 / E7 / ||

or this:

| C7 / / / | A7 / / / | Dmin / A7 / | Dmin / / / |
| F / F#° / | C / A7 / | D7 / / / | G7 / / / ||

Both of the above are eight-bar blues and very different in style. What's more, they are only two of the variations on the twelve-bar norm available. You'll encounter many more if you explore the repertoire thoroughly.

"Really, before that kind of period, there were blues ballads that could take a number of chord structures, but they were primary using three chords, but not in a twelve-bar structure. It wasn't until later that they established it into a twelve-bar form. But of course Bessie Smith is also considered to be a jazz singer, and at

▲ Track 61

▲ Track 62

that time there was no difference between blues and jazz; it was all the same. It was just music that people played. It wasn't until prohibition came to the fore, during the '20s with the speakeasy clubs, that blues began to get hot and jazz got hotter. But the sources they used were ragtime and blues, and ragtime probably has more relevance to the African roots than blues does, because blues is not really African; it was the one music that was invented in America by black people. You can trace all other music to European sources, but the blues was invented in America by black people. The melodies are definitely tinged with what you might hear in Irish folk music or any other European folk music. Even in Russian folk music they use the same ambiguous major/ minor third.

"It's the rhythms that have come from Africa, if anything, and certainly if you listen to ragtime and Blind Blake you'll hear them. In fact, there's enough material for a whole article on the Gullah Tribe from Senegal who lived in the Georgia Sea Islands, South Carolina, and had a language called Gichi. It was the part in America where the culture was allowed to be retained. Everywhere else, people were split up and divided and they weren't even allowed to bang drums because of the so-called 'sinister implications'. The rhythm for all the ragtime type of stuff and syncopation emanated from there. That's why the Charleston – which is just above the Georgia South Sea Islands – sounds like it does. I'd love to go back and try to see if I can find any origins. I'm told it's all gone, but it wouldn't surprise me that, if you went with the right attitude, you might find something left because, whilst it's an island, it's a hell of a big island. I think there were probably about two million slaves on that one island. It was huge." *King Rollo*

Melody

There tends to be an over-simplification in this particular quarter of blues mythology, too. This has

a lot to do with the belief that the minor pentatonic

A minor pentatonic

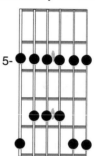

is a cure-all for blues-melody-related afflictions. Not so. Neither is the blues scale. Sorry, life's just like that sometimes.

Let's take another look at the minor pentatonic scale: The thing about this durable little scale is that it does fit just about every blues situation you can name. You can quite happily play the scale up and down in the same key as the blues you're playing and nothing is going to sound too wrong. It just won't sound too right, either. If you think of the minor pentatonic as being the lowest common denominator of melodic tools, you'd be about right. Think about this every time you're slightly unwilling to learn any other scales!

In order to make the minor pentatonic more useful, we've got to add a few things. Don't worry, this shouldn't hurt a bit.

The reason why we have to make a few additions is the nature of the derivation of blues music in general. Unless you're really interested in all the musicological aspects of blues archaeology (and if you are, I'd recommend a book called *Early Jazz* by Gunther Schuller), you won't want me to go into it here. Just take everything at face value once again.

The first addition we'll make is the flat fifth. This is known as a *blue note* and also crops up a lot in jazz harmony. The flat fifth gained itself quite a reputation in the Middle Ages, when, for some reason, the learned men of the church considered that it must be representative of the Devil. Don't ask me why, but it was something to do with the fact that the flat fifth sits halfway along the chromatic scale and doesn't sound very nice in its basic form. Try it.

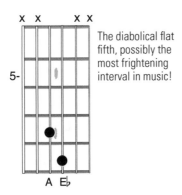

The diabolical flat fifth, possibly the most frightening interval in music!

A E♭

Every time anything so perfect turns out to be an ugly little mother has just got to be the work of the horned one, hasn't it, boys and girls? So they banned it from church music (seriously – it was known as the *Diabolus in musica*, the Devil in music), until Bach managed to sneak it back in. And, as we know…

"If Bach did it, it's OK."

So now you know. But the blues is also known as "the Devil's music", and so we welcome this little demon into the minor pentatonic with open arms. Here it is:

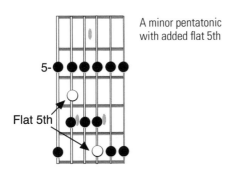

A minor pentatonic with added flat 5th

Flat 5th

If you listen to the transformed result, the presence of the flat fifth actually smoothes out the sound of the scale a little. Listen again to the two notes it connects in the scale and hopefully you'll see what I mean.

The next addition is actually quite a surprise in a minor scale: the major third. If you recall when we looked at triads, it's the third note in the scale, containing the basic gender-related information and determining whether the scale is major or minor. So what happens when both of them turn up in the same scale? Actually, it poses another question: How can a minor scale sound right over major chords? If you look at the chord arrangements listed above, you'll notice that they're both major for the most part, and yet I'm recommending a minor scale over the top of them. How does this work?

Again, it's all to do with the nature of the blues, and once again I'm not going to go into too much detail. (I mean, I find this sort of thing interesting, but people I've been trapped in lifts with in the past haven't.) Let's just say that it's not so much a case of having both the minor and major genders present in the scale at the same time; it's more a case of having a single, indeterminately gendered third present in the scale. Here it is:

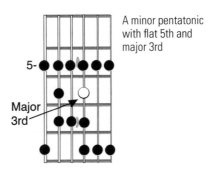

A minor pentatonic with flat 5th and major 3rd

Major 3rd

In practice, blues guitarists bend this note to achieve the "genderless third" sound of the blues. Another convention, however, comes to us from the piano, where obviously bending is out of the question. This convention dictates that, after the minor third is played, the major third is hammered on immediately, resulting in a slurred third, which sounds a lot less disgusting than you might imagine. Here's an example:

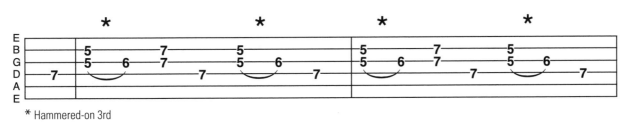

* Hammered-on 3rd

The Slurred Third

Sometimes, the blues scale is written down with just these two additions to a straight minor pentatonic, and in my opinion that's very far from the real story. The trouble with scales in general is that they're very much after the fact, if you see what I mean. For example, we're agreed that music existed long before the academics got hold of it in the name of analysis, aren't we? They had to look at the different music forms and write down which notes were used commonly in each, and in that way they came up with the common denominator: the scale. It's my belief that a lot of folk music (that's what we're talking about when we consider the blues; Robert Johnson didn't go to music school) actually resists any attempt to tame it as part of a scientific survey. It's a far more elusive thing than that.

The trouble is we need a handrail like a scale to guide us through the stylistic jungle, and so we have to present something. As I say, I think that simply adding the major/minor third and flat fifth isn't really telling the whole story, so I'll go out on a limb and say that the melodic content of an awful lot of blues melody comprises a fusion between major and minor pentatonic scales, with the flat fifth thrown in for good luck. Consider this:

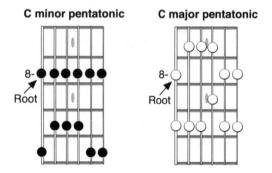

C minor pentatonic **C major pentatonic**

This shows the major and minor pentatonic scales sitting side by side. If we want to make one scale out of both of them, this is what we end up with:

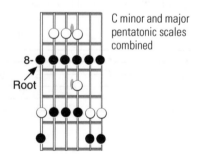

C minor and major pentatonic scales combined

If you want an analysis, here it is in the key of C:

$$
\begin{array}{l}
C \; D \; E \; G \; A \\
+ \; C \; E\flat \; F \; G \; B\flat \\
+ \; \underline{G\flat} \\
C \; D \; E\flat \; E \; F \; G\flat \; G \; A \; B\flat \; C
\end{array}
$$

The formula above is for the C-major pentatonic plus the C-minor pentatonic, plus the flat fifth. The result of that equation would be this, from a fretboard perspective:

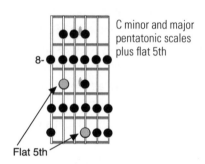

C minor and major pentatonic scales plus flat 5th

Flat 5th

Now, the problem here is that we've ended up with a nine-note scale, which is a little extravagant, in musical terms, so maybe it's best to think of both the third(s) and fifth(s) as single "slurred" or "non-defined" entities. So here it is again with the "slurs" added:

C D E♭/E F G♭/G A B♭ C

And now we're back to the good old seven-note scale again. What's more, it's actually recognisable as some sort of scale this time because of its resemblance to a kind of perverse dominant-seventh scale. Observe:

C Dominant Seventh Scale

C D E F G A B♭ C

C Blues Scale

C D E♭/E F G♭/G A B♭ C

So I like to think of the blues scale as being of the dominant family with slurred third and fifth – often called the *blue notes*. This sits quite nicely with jazz theory, too.

The only remaining problem here is that it doesn't

sound too much like blues when you play it cold, whereas the minor pentatonic with the flat fifth perhaps does. My argument here is that the major scale doesn't sound much like Beethoven's ninth symphony when you play it, either. See my point? So, given that it's not exactly too useful as an aural nudge into the sound of the blues (but, like I say, which scale is?), I think that it's a much more accurate portrayal of the blues scale than is usually written. Certainly by learning this you won't be surprised to find ninths and sixths cropping up in the blues, whereas if you considered the minor pentatonic alone you'd be forgiven for being confused.

"I think the definitive thing about the blues is that it's nothing to do with playing. You either have the blues or you don't. But you can always recall those feelings because they're so vivid. You don't have to have the blues the time you're singing the blues, but there has to have been a period in your life that was so shitty that you could really get down in your soul." *King Rollo*

Jazz

"As a teenager, all I wanted to do was play jazz; rock came a bit later for me. I listened to all the American jazz players and played in a jazz club. Rock and R&B actually came much later. I just started out by learning hundreds of standards." *Andy Summers*

It's widely thought that you can't play jazz without learning to play blues first, and it's certainly true that much that is jazz emanates directly from the blues. If you study the history of the development of both music genres, you'll see how they grew up together and were – at one historical point, at least – almost inseparable.

From a theoretical point of view, too, it's helpful to look at my personal interpretation of the blues scale and look forward into jazz, seeing this as perhaps another form of "altered dominant" thinking.

"The route that I took in jazz was more a melodic one which stems back to the time that I thought of improvisation as playing my own melodies over a chord sequence. So I do think melodically. I don't think about scales; I know them, and over the years I've learned the theory and harmony, but to me it's just been making music.

"One of the things that can happen is that you take up an instrument to make music and you become tied up with the technicalities of the instrument itself and the music is put into the background. That happens a hell of a lot in jazz, sad to say." *Martin Taylor*

Harmony

"People always seem to have the same problems, like playing over changes and getting jazz timing or feel, but particularly what you do over chord changes. Playing with other people, listening and so on seem to be perennial problems. People don't seem to have too much of a problem with technique, getting their scales down and all that." *John Etheridge on learning jazz*

I realise that jazz chord charts might seem to resemble advanced mathematics if you're not used to them, and this is something that puts off a lot of people straight away. I'm also aware that jazz is slagged off for notoriously being "16 bars in search of a melody", with the jazz quartet often being defined as four reasons to reach for a blunt instrument, but a lot of this criticism is very unfair. Playing jazz is a very rewarding experience for a musician and all it takes is a little understanding.

The first thing to do is to buy yourself a good chord book (you're going to need it) and a *Real Book*. A *Real Book* is a collection of several hundred jazz standards with the correct chord changes and melody lines inside. In my early jazz days, they used to be called *Fake Books* because the idea was that, if you were acquainted with the way music was written down and could read a basic chord chart, you could fake your way through anything! But these books were usually illegal, in the sense that no copyright had been paid to the original authors of the music they contained. I had one that was made up of photocopies (very naughty) and was invaluable if I found myself on a jazz gig and someone called for a tune I didn't know (which, incidentally, was most of the time. I have one of the worst memories for tunes in the world and have trouble matching tunes to titles, even with material I've written myself. But I digress.)

Eventually, *Fake Books* became real when publishing dues were paid and the same essential content became published by recognised companies. They're invaluable in terms of researching your basic source material, because just about every jazz standard you'll come across in the early stages will be in them.

If you're interested in jazz, I'm assuming that this interest will have come from somewhere, probably from listening to some of the great jazz guitarists and wishing you could come up with a half-decent solo in the style of, say, Wes Montgomery or a passable chord-melody treatment in the style of Joe Pass. If this is the case, you'll probably be fairly well acquainted with some of the popular jazz standards, at least by name, so it would be fairly easy to put together a list of tunes from the jazz-standard mainstream – you'll certainly need to look at tunes like Gershwin's 'I Got Rhythm' and 'Summertime'. Plumbing the depths of other great songwriters such as Van Heusen, Cole Porter, Rodgers and Hart and Hoagy Carmichael would be a good idea, too.

You'll need a list of about five standards to begin with, and the first thing you should do is learn the melodies and chord arrangements. This will give you the bare bones of the song and is really all you need as a platform to take you to the next level.

When I say, "Learn the melody," I mean really *learn* it. Learn to play it in the written key (to begin with) and memorise it. Don't write it out in tab or rely on reading the music. You want these tunes in your head, not on a piece of paper.

"Know the song. Know the song first, the words and what it means to you, and then the guitar will come in behind it. I don't think that the guitar is more important than the song. So, if you can accompany the song and enhance the words, that's the best technique. The guitar will come as you know the song better." *John Hammond*

Learn the chord arrangement alongside the melody. This is where your jazz-friendly chord book will come in handy. There will be chords involved that will be new to you, but if you've read the "Painless Music Theory I" chapter you'll be able to identify their basic families at sight. The most daunting thing will be the fact that so many of the chords will bear extensions. In jazz, you're often dealing with reasonably dense harmony, where we're not talking basic triads; we're delving a bit deeper. You're unlikely to come across too many straight major or minor chords, as the fashion in jazz is to extend virtually everything to at least a seventh. In other words, you're more likely to find major sevenths, minor sevenths and so on as standard. But it's the dominant family that becomes really scary.

Even when the chord arrangement calls for dominant-type voicings, they're unlikely to be straight ninths, 13ths or whatever. You'll find chromatic extensions aplenty and many of the dominants are likely to be suffixed by either sharp or flat ninths or sharp or flat fifths. If you recall, I referred to these chords as being highly coloured or spiced and very specific in the way that they support a melody. Playing through any of your chosen standards will show you how commonplace extended dominant harmony is in jazz. But don't let this put you off! It might look like a seriously daunting task to begin with, but it gets easier as you become more familiar with the fretboard and chords in general. You'll find yourself having to refer to your chord book less and less as time goes on, especially if you adopt a system like the CAGED idea outlined in the "Left-Hand Development" chapter. You'll begin to see patterns on the fretboard and spot how chords relate to each other and things generally will begin to make more sense. Understanding the basic idea of chord formulae (ie C7 = C E G B♭) will help your progress along nicely, too, but to begin with I'd recommend that you take everything at face value and leave the understanding bit until later.

Melody

"In jazz, it isn't enough to have a good melody; you've got to have an interesting enough harmonic structure to mess around with. If you've got a ballad with a really, fantastically strong melody, then I would keep that and reharmonise it, in the same way that an arranger would with an orchestra. But you've got to have an interesting structure to begin with." *Martin Taylor*

People often ask the question, "What's the scale that you use to play jazz solos?", and the answer is a frustrating one because there are many that could be said to come into play. But remember that scales do not equal music, in the same way that the alphabet isn't literature. Scales are a resource from which music is drawn, that's all, and so, even if you could play every scale in the book, you still might not grasp what jazz is all about.

The problem is usually that a player and would-be jazz student has familiarised himself with the minor pentatonic scale and has found – sometimes to his considerable cost – that it doesn't fit over anything in the jazz repertoire. Well, hardly anything, anyway. This fact alone has persuaded a lot of people to give up and agree that jazz is better kept away from civilisation in general. But I've found that so many people approach jazz as if it's some kind of arcane science and place jazz musicians on a level with alchemists or practitioners of the Black Arts.

In all honesty, here you're better off following a similar course to the one I suggested you adopt for exploring jazz harmony: do a lot of listening and take everything at face value, in the early stages. You'll need some transcribed solos – preferably matched up to your chosen list of standards – by either guitarists or sax players, and an afternoon spent battling away with search engines on the Internet should throw up quite a few transcriptions virtually free of charge. (I only recommend this course of action, as opposed to actually going out and buying them in book form, because there is so little of this kind of thing published in book form.)

Without a doubt, though, it's listening that will do you the most good, even if it has the sole effect of occasionally setting you off in a new direction. When we talked about ear training earlier on, I suggested that you'd have to change your listening habits so that music was promoted from being background noise to holy scripture as part of your practice routine. This is especially good advice if you're intent on cracking the jazz code.

"Get the sound in your head by listening to records. Find the music you really like, listen to it all the time and then one day you'll be walking down the street and the record will just play itself back in your head. Half the battle is knowing how it goes." *Bob Brozman*

Listen to anything you can get your hands on, but I especially believe that you can learn virtually anything you need to know about jazz soloing from listening to Charlie Parker. This is, in effect, going back to the roots of modern-day jazz soloing – heresy, I know, because I'm writing an awful lot of jazz history off by saying this, but it was Parker who really set the course for modern jazz, in that he made the whole of the chromatic scale available for use melodically, whereas previously jazz was, in the main, largely diatonic (ie it stuck to the prevailing key quite faithfully and didn't use extensions like sharp or flat ninths).

Parker's jazz-guitar equivalent was Charlie Christian, who exploded the myth that decreed that the guitar was part of the rhythm section and much too quiet to take solos. When Christian got his hands on an electric guitar, that all changed.

Listen to Django Reinhardt, too, who pioneered the sound of European jazz with his unique take on Gypsy jazz soloing. It's fair to say that Django is about as far away as you can get from bebop-influenced players like Joe Pass, Wes Montgomery, Barney Kessell, Herb Ellis and co, and although he's not to everyone's taste, he's definitely worth a listen in order to get some historical perspective.

"I listen to my favourite records that I used to look to when I first got excited about it all, now and again. The hardest thing to get out of those records is why they play the way they do – the emotion behind it, the passion and so on. I think you have to listen to a record and grab hold of that spirit and then it takes you to how, why and what made them play the notes that they do, whether it's a flurry or whether it's one pretty singing note just to put a dab of colour on a piece of paper. If you listen to a song that way and try to play it that way, it's magical. That's where you get that spirit from." *Robert Cray*

Chord Melody

"The main weak spot I find present in players who come to clinics is melodic concept. I think technique has risen to the point where so many players out there can really, *really* play, but it's very rare that you hear a mature player, someone who can take you in and out, who has a sense of melody and who can really phrase." *John Petrucci*

If this particular area of jazz guitar appeals to you, then read on. Learning about chord melody effectively begins in just the same way, with learning standards from both melodic and harmonic points of view. It's just that you've got to learn to combine the two simultaneously.

Obviously, I haven't got the space here to do anything more than give you an approximate outline of the work that playing chord-melody guitar entails. It calls very heavily upon disciplines more common to classical guitar – indeed, any self-accompaniment style shares some of its basic technique with classical guitar – so it's not a bad idea to consider having a few lessons from a classical teacher, who will be able to guide you through the fundamentals of right-hand positioning and fingering.

If you want to go it alone, I would recommend that you adopt Mauro Giuliani's *Studies For Guitar* as part of your daily practice routine. This is a book dedicated to the development of both hands and was largely responsible for my own right hand becoming fit and able when I began to take fingerstyle guitar more seriously. The exercises are quite simple (and similar to the ones I've detailed in the "Right-Hand Development" chapter) and based around C-major and G7 chords, so the left hand can take things fairly easy. It's just that the fingering for the right hand becomes ever more complex. I made a game out of it and added about half a dozen exercises (there are 120) every couple of weeks. The game was that, if I made a mistake, I went back to the beginning and started again. I did that for ages and it had the effect of bringing my right hand up to speed nicely. It's invaluable stuff for learning some of the right-hand antics involved in chord-melody playing.

Apart from the actual physical side of practising, you'd do well to check out as many players as possible who are self-accompanists or soloists right across the style spectrum. I'd recommend listening to Joe Pass, Martin Taylor, Charlie Byrd, Ike Isaacs, Tuck Andress and other similar players on the jazz front, but also don't forget guys like Chet Atkins, Tommy Emmanuel, Michael Hedges, Thomas Leeb, Antonio Forcione and Eric Roche, too. Remember, everyone who plays the instrument well can inspire you, completely irrespective of style.

ALTERED TUNINGS

"At first, I didn't know about open tunings, and then I got a Mel Bay steel-guitar book (I actually had a little Fender lap slide with six strings and a single pick-up) and that's how I learned about G and E tuning. That was when I started to experiment, especially with E, because of the common notes with standard tuning. That way, it gave me something to work with that I could relate to as a point of reference. Then I took what I learned from the lap steel and applied it to the bottleneck style." *Sonny Landreth*

Another variable that the acoustic guitar can throw in your path is altered tunings. These can be anything from dropping your low E string down to D for a more profound bass sound to retuning all of the strings completely. You'd be forgiven for thinking that this is an introduction to a whole new world of pain, as regular tuning can be quite enough to overheat even the most sturdy cranium, but you'd be surprised at some of the benefits available to you with just the simplest tweak of the tuning pegs.

OK, Drop 'Em

To begin with, let's see how retuning a single string can add quite a lot to the simplest of chord arrangements.

Drop D

This involves dropping your low E string to D. To begin with, it's advisable to use an electronic tuner to help you take the plunge. Then, just for good measure, check it

against the open fourth string to hear the effect. Now play the D chord below:

D maj chord in drop-D tuning

Exercise 1   D A D A D F♯

▲ Track 66

If you compare this with the more regular version of D major, which employs only the top four strings, I hope you'll agree that this version sounds far more full – majestic, even. It gives you access to some totally new-sounding ideas based on well-worn themes, like this one:

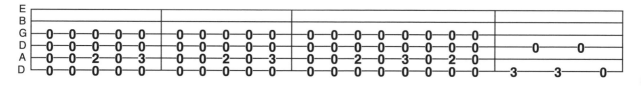

▲ Track 67

Drop D can give a new dimension to any chord in which D is a constituent part – in other words, if there's a D

in the chord somewhere, try it in this tuning and hear what it sounds like.

Open G

Quite often, you'll find the guitar tuned to a chord, especially for slide playing. An open-G tuning means that your guitar is tuned like this:

Bass	D
	G
	D
	G
	B
Treble	D

If you refer back to the "Painless Music Theory" chapters, you'll be able to work out that we've got the chord of G fairly well represented here. Remember the formula?

$$G = G \quad B \quad D$$
$$1 \quad 3 \quad 5$$

Take a look at the tuning and you'll see how the recipe for the chord of G has been spread over the open strings.

This, of course, means that barre chords in this type of tuning turn into really finger-friendly little devices, as every fret will give you a major chord with just one finger barring the strings, so you'd have major-chord forms like these available to you:

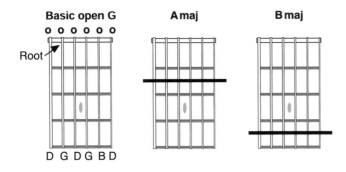

Naturally, a capo can come in really handy here for changing open G to open anything at the flick of a switch.

On the CD, you can hear what this tuning sounds like demonstrated with a couple of simple fingerpicked ideas.

Open D

Open D calls for you to retune like this:

Bass	D
	A
	D
	F#
	A
Treble	D

This is in accordance with the chord formula for D major, which tells us this:

$$D = D \quad F\# \quad A$$
$$1 \quad 3 \quad 5$$

Once again, barre chords are luxuriously easy, a capo will transport you to any key of your choosing and even the simplest of fingerpicking ideas begins to sound very exotic indeed.

In theory, you can tune to any open chord you like. I tend to shy away from those that call for strings to be tuned up in pitch, but obviously it's a two-way street inasmuch as strings can go up as well as down to suit the tuning in hand. It's just a matter of squeamish preference with me that I don't like torturing my trusty acoustic by placing it under any additional strain!

Not all tunings need necessarily be tuned to a chord, however. Possibly the most famous "folk" tuning of all is very close to open-D tuning, but not quite.

DADGAD

Believe it or not, that's not some sort of Gaelic swear word; it's actually style of guitar tuning that calls, not unexpectedly, for the strings to be retuned like this:

Bass	D
	A
	D
	G
	A
Treble	D

I said that it was close to an open-D tuning, and if you compare the two you'll see what I mean. DADGAD doesn't conform to open-chord thinking in this way; it actually sounds more like a D suspended chord:

$$D \, sus4 = \begin{array}{ccc} D & G & A \\ 1 & 4 & 5 \end{array}$$

This is also known as a *modal tuning*, more for the way it sounds than anything else, and is a favourite of Led Zeppelin's Jimmy Page, who played tracks like 'Kashmir' and 'Black Mountain Side' using its atmospheric charms.

Sometimes it's good to tune to something like DADGAD and try to play in a familiar music form, like the 'DADGAD Blues' on the CD. Here are the chord voicings I'm using. See if you can put together something like it yourself.

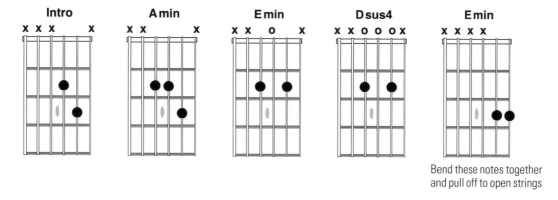

Bend these notes together
and pull off to open strings

Combine these chords with the basic "drop-D boogie" idea. (Drop D shares the same tuning as DADGAD on the lower three strings.)

The key is experimentation. Even if you're quite an old hand in regular tuning, any retuning is going to throw you off course a little. It's a good thing for your ear because it makes you explore the new tuning aurally at first. In fact, any chord form you try will be a shot in the dark, and it becomes a real test of your musicianship.

Obviously, as far as tunings are concerned, you're only limited by your imagination and the practicality of the new configuration of open pitches. Each new tuning means new chord shapes and scale patterns to learn, and I'll admit that I don't use too many myself (although drop D and DADGAD are my personal favourites), but if you hear a piece that defies all working out, that literally doesn't conform to any known reference points on the guitar that you've learned so far, the chances are that a tuning is being used.

"I tune my normal six strings in perfect fourths: E A D G C F. [On the eight string], I have two more strings; I'm going down in fourths so I have

a B and a low F♯, so I go from F♯ to F." *Stanley Jordan on tuning his eight-string guitar*

"I wrote 'Sultans Of Swing' on a National in open tuning and it was a completely different tune. When I got the Strat, it sounded so different that it became another song." *Mark Knopfler*

"I use G tuning a lot [DGDGBD, bass to treble]. The guitar playing on The Beatles' 'Blackbird' is basically an exercise in diatonic harmony in G tuning. I also use altered tunings where I might go to G minor or G suspended; the D family of tunings like D major, which is DADF♯AD; sometimes I use DADGAD. I also play in a family of C tunings. There's CGCGCE, but the E can be E♭ or D for a Celtic sound. The top string can sometimes be C, too, double-C tuning, which means that you've got no minor third, and that cuts away a lot of the bullshit." *Bob Brozman*

"Sometimes I'll just detune the guitar to DADGAD because it's one of my favourite tunings. It's great for folky sort of stuff and I know a few shapes in that domain." *Dominic Miller*

"I use a different one for 'Down Down' and a different one for 'Whatever You Want'. I just don't like the idea of people standing onstage dropping the Es down to the D and, 'Hey, look at me tune this guitar!' People don't need to see that, so I'll just grab another one. But I also don't like changes of guitar all over the shop. I try to keep those down to the minimum. I think, again, from an audience's point of view, 'Oh, he's off to change his guitar. What's the matter with him?' It's like, 'Look at me! I can play this one as well.' I don't think they're interested." *Status Quo's Francis Rossi on tunings*

"I had a friend named Bob Silverman at college, where I went for a year, and Bob was a much more accomplished guitar player than I was and he showed me an open-D tuning. It was like a revelation: 'So that's how they get that sound!' Just odd things like that. I'm sure every guitar player says the same things. We all have a friend called Harry who shows us things. It's a traditional art form, and you pick things up just hanging out, I guess.

"I use open E and open A. It's like a D tuning taken up to E and a G tuning taken up to A. I do that for my voice. It's the key which will enhance my voice better." *John Hammond*

"I learned about tunings from Ralph McTell, really. One soggy afternoon outside the Folk Cottage – I think we were going to do some duets that night – he dropped his E string down to D and, coming up through jazz, it was a thing that I hadn't ever seen. I mean, I was the guy who tried to play 'Sleepwalk' in regular tuning on an acoustic without a bottleneck! So Ralph showed me drop-D tuning and I thought, 'Aaaah!' All of a sudden, things began to make sense and I took it on from there. What I wanted to find was better bass lines than the ones I could play in normal tuning. Drop D seems to enlarge the bottom end of the guitar because, if you want to play a D without dropping the E string, you're ten notes short of the octave – you can't get another D at the bottom. So, by dropping the D, you've almost given yourself another octave. I know it's only a tone down, but it sort of blossoms at the bottom, I think. One pet theory is that that's where guitars are meant to be, anyway. Whoever discovered standard tuning did a great job, but it's not as precious as a lot of people think it is." *Michael Chapman*

"Now I use an awful lot of open tunings which [are] similar to the way a banjo is tuned. A true bluegrass banjo is tuned to an open G chord and I use a variation of that on my guitar, which gives me a much fuller sound, and I've been able to adapt how I play chords on a banjo to the way I play them on guitar. When you hear [some of] the stuff I've recorded…you'll think that I'm playing fingerstyle, but I'm not; I'm using a variation of pick and fingers. It's just something I've developed that I'm comfortable with. I couldn't teach it in a million years!" *Tim Rose*

"It's mostly standard tuning. The only time I change is tuning the bass E string to D occasionally. I've yet to discover DADGAD and things like that. I love the sound of it, but I'm having enough trouble with standard tuning!" *Tommy Emmanuel*

NYLON-STRING GUITAR

"I always thought that, to get a good sound on a steel-string guitar, you have to spend a lot more money, and when you're a teenager you don't have too much money, but you can still get a decent sound from a reasonably cheap nylon-string." Antonio Forcione

I don't think that the quietly voiced nylon-string guitar ever saw the day when it might take to the stage alongside its far more forthright and boisterous descendants, the electric and acoustic guitars, but modern technology has seen developments in the area of nylon-string guitar manufacture to the extent that it's now commonplace for them to come with onboard electronics that allow their voices to be heard everywhere from small clubs to sports stadiums.

Designs vary from the very rock 'n' roll, solid-body nylon-string to the more conventional-looking Spanish-style model. With the latter, the electronics are hidden away from view, and to all intents and purposes they look exactly like the pure acoustic version, but there's a transducer pick-up lurking under the bridge saddle and volume and tone controls cut into the upper side, along with a battery compartment for onboard power.

If you're used to playing steel-string guitar, you might find yourself needing to make some minor adjustments to your technique, but not too many. In fact, there are probably only two areas to consider:

Sounding The Strings

With steel-string guitar, we've seen that the convention is to either fingerpick or use a plectrum. What's more, the fingerpicking regime is pretty much a case of using upstrokes with the fingers and downstrokes with the thumb. With classical guitar, this process is a lot more specific in that there are two basic types of playing stroke.

Free Stroke

This is essentially what you might have been using to play fingerstyle, in any case. It's called free stroke because the finger plucks the string and follows through in preparation to do so again for the next note it's destined to play.

▲ Track 73

Rest Stroke

This is similar to free stroke, the main difference being that, after the finger has plucked the string, it comes to rest on the next adjacent string. In other words you use the string "above" the one you've just plucked as a sort of buffer to bring it to a halt.

▲ Track 74

You might not think there'd be too much difference between the two types, but you'd be surprised. (There's an example on the CD – tracks 73 and 74.) The rest stroke is effective for playing that kind of romantic, sweet-sounding nylon-string guitar, and so it's a technique worth mastering if you're into that kind of thing.

Vibrato

As we saw in the "Left-Hand Development" chapter, classical vibrato differs from rock or blues vibrato in that it's far more subtle. Obviously, this particular form of vibrato technique is natural to the nylon-string guitar and is worth looking at if you want authenticity.

"I played classical guitar in the States prior to joining The Police, barely touching an electric, so I spent years on an acoustic instrument prior

137

to The Police. I've always had one. It will probably come as a surprise, but people don't know everything about you, do they?" *Andy Summers*

In terms of build, the nylon-string guitar's neck joins the body at the twelfth fret, meaning that access is limited to the upper register, but some models swerve away from convention to the extent that they have a cutaway – just like you'd expect to find on a steel-string guitar – which takes this into account. Fingerboards on classical guitars are usually wider, too, and so you might find that this interferes with the ease of transition between the two types of instrument.

The question of whether you play with pick or fingers on this type of guitar is the same, although you'd expect perhaps that convention would demand that fingerstyle is the only possible route to follow, in deference to the classical guitar's heritage (although some classical guitar was played using a plectrum as long ago as the 17th century). My own take on this situation is to use whichever form of string-sounding apparatus you're used to. It really doesn't matter too much.

Tonally, the nylon-string guitar has a lot to offer, but in my experience you have to try harder to obtain the best results. In general, picking near the bridge produces a harsher, more metallic tone, whereas picking near the fingerboard makes for a much sweeter response. This, of course, is true of most types of guitar, but it seems especially true on the nylon-string.

Another difference between steel- and nylon-string guitar is that the dynamic range of the nylon-string is a slightly strange beast.

"The main problem with guitar is that the dynamics and the sustain are not relative to the loudness or the range of the instrument. In other words, if you play a quiet note, you get X, the sound. But if you play the same note loudly, you should get X-plus and you don't. You get a lot of extra percussive pluck at the front of the note, but you don't get a lot of extra sustain. The sustain doesn't carry on longer, nor is the sustain itself louder. It's in the nature of the traditional fan-strutting of the instrument that when you pluck louder you get a louder pluck sound but you get comparatively less increase in the volume of the sustain. That's the crucial point. Play a piano note softly and forget the split second you bang the note. Just listen to the sustain. Then do it very loudly and you'll hear the sustain is much louder as well." *John Williams*

Many players have chosen to include the more sombre sounds of nylon-string guitar in their music: Dominic Miller from Sting's band is a prime example, having recorded two excellent solo albums using his solid-body nylon-string guitar as well as using the instrument liberally in his gigs with Sting.

"It's actually got quite a narrow neck, almost like an acoustic guitar's, with a curved fingerboard, and classical guitars aren't curved at all. It's almost like playing an electric. It's very bright, very responsive, and so the dynamic range is great; you can play soft or hard and it really comes through.

"It can take years to put your stamp on a guitar like a Rodriguez. It's usually very hard to get a sound on a classical guitar. In the studio, it's just straight DI. There's nothing – zero on the desk. We don't use any compression." *Dominic Miller on his solid-body, nylon-string P-Project guitar from Fernandez*

Antonio Forcione is another artist who has taken the nylon string into new areas and even invented a variation on the classical-guitar theme:

"A couple of years ago, I was in Madrid and I found an oud in a shop and I thought I would buy it and try to play it because I just loved that sound. So I bought it – it was my birthday! – and I came back home and for the whole week I tried to play it. I had just reached the point where I thought I was really going to pursue it and learn to play it. I had a difficulty on my right hand more than my left because the spacing of the strings near the bridge is a lot greater than the guitar. I thought it would be very hard for me to get used to it and I would never really be able to acquire the technique or speed. Therefore I left it for a whole week but started to think, 'What about a guitar with no frets?' I had no idea what it would sound like, so I got one of my old guitars out of the loft, got a hammer and screwdriver and started taking the frets out. My girlfriend came home while I was doing it and she thought I'd gone mad! I started to play it and, although the guitar wasn't a great one, I could see the potential straight away. I could hear something that I felt comfortable with. So I made a phone call to Barnes & Mullins, who import Spanish guitars in the UK, and asked them if they could find me a cutaway guitar which was quite good and take the frets off. They sent it here and I started playing it and I was really enthusiastic and thought it sounded great. It already had a Fishman pick-up on it.

"So I called [guitar builder and repairer] Bill Puplett and I told him about the idea and asked him if he could add some strings which would make a chord, because the idea was from the oud and the strings were from the raga – the Indian drone idea – and I wanted to mix both things. I couldn't play chords, because once you have no frets you can't really play chords; it's really hard. So Bill said, 'Come along and we'll design it.' He's done a really fine job, adding eight more strings and doing such a neat job. The drone strings I tuned to a sort of A7 without the third,

so it can be used in D or A. I started writing a tune called 'Indian Cafe' and the more I heard it, the more I thought of Trilok Gurtu. He had heard my album *Acoustic Revenge* and liked it and we were due to play together, but it never happened. So I contacted him again and he agreed to play on my album. I used the new guitar on a couple of tracks on the new album. I've called the guitar the Ouddan." *Antonio Forcione*

The Studio

In the recording studio, the miking up of acoustic instruments is a skilled job. Mic position is critical, and just a few centimetres can make the difference between a good and a bad sound.

"We spent hours miking [a Rodriguez classical] up in the studio using two or three mics. We were in a big room, so we'd have a close mic, one of those expensive Sony ones, then we'd use another by my fingers and an ambient mic somewhere in the room. You'd be surprised what a difference it makes just moving the mic a half-inch either way." *Dominic Miller*

Just to give you some idea about how the voice of the acoustic guitar can be enhanced in the recording studio, the CD gives you a few examples of different treatments from the array of effects currently available.

▲ Track 75-8

PERFORMANCE

"I played in sub-zero weather and I played in places that were so hot I was gonna cancel it, and you look out at these people and there's water running down their faces or people with overcoats on and they think that much of you to come out and hear you play, I think you owe them 110 per cent of yourself." Buddy Guy

As far as "performance" goes, I consider playing with anybody listening to be a performance, so don't skip this chapter just because you thought I meant playing at Carnegie Hall!

Obviously, there are different levels of performance – playing to a couple of friends in your living room wouldn't require too much adjustment to your playing habits, other than anything that's required to help you overcome any sense of embarrassment or stagefright.

Curing the heebie-jeebies is well outside the parameters of this book, but I will say that it gets better with time and experience. Performing in public – even family gatherings – can be nerve-racking at first, but this will go as you become more and more sure of what you're doing. There are some for whom paralysis from nerves has to be worked on separately, and some people are never cured. Maybe actual performance just isn't for them. I've found among many of my own pupils that the desire to get up and play in public offsets any straightforward feelings of nervousness, while for others performance is never an aim.

Practice Versus Performance

I was once told by a very wise guitar tutor the difference between practising a piece and performing it. He said that you can take three weeks to learn a piece and six months to learn how to perform it. It took me ages before I discovered what he meant and I made the mistake of trying to perform pieces I knew how to play but didn't know well enough to

perform in public. It's a very fine dividing line, but I'll try to explain.

To use another parallel, my driving instructor once told me that our first job was to get me past my driving test and then he'd teach me how to drive. I was puzzled by this, too, but having passed my test, I realised how few real road skills I actually possessed. It's the same with music: merely knowing the chords of a piece doesn't mean you're able to perform it in public; there are a few more subtle things that have to happen first. For a start, you have to be able to inject some sort of passion into the way you play or your audience is going to hear a "cold" reading of whatever it is you're playing. You don't want something you play to sound like a lesson you've just copied down from a blackboard; you have to learn to interpret and personalise it.

If you go to a gig to watch someone, you can forgive almost everything as long as the performance itself speaks to you in some way, as long as it involves you emotionally somehow and you find yourself moved by it. I've been to gigs where the sound was very poor, there was no seating and I had to stand (which I hate doing) and take part in a form of tag-team wrestling just to get to the bar, and yet I'd come away from the gig feeling ecstatic, knowing that I'd just seen something very special indeed.

Remember that no one is going to award you points for technical merit, either, and so buffing up some sort of party piece will go straight over the heads of most members of the music-loving public. They couldn't give a fig about guitars or guitarists; they're just tools of the trade and a means to an end. They're right, too; as musicians, we sometimes forget that an actual performance is bigger than the choice of material on your set-list. It has to contain something else and it has to be entertaining or you just haven't got a show.

"I've thrown both my shoes at a Guitar Craft student performing in a rough redneck bar in West Virginia. He was a Los Angeles attorney and it was so much performed in his sleep that I threw both of my shoes at him consecutively. So he looked up at me, took off his shoes and threw them back." *Robert Fripp*

The Live Stage
"I find playing small gigs really hard because you're so close to everyone and you're exposed and your weaknesses are exposed, too, and yet it's much more rewarding." *Dominic Miller*

Playing acoustic guitar live is a thing that has only really been made possible at pub-gig level via electro-acoustics. Once upon a time (and I'm not going too far back here), playing a song that called for an acoustic was simply not worth it. An average pub band couldn't afford to stump up for an acoustic-guitar mic and so, after maybe trying every other conceivable option available – using another vocal mic to pick up the acoustic, strapping a pick-up on the acoustic, getting hold of one of the early transducer "bug" pick-ups and finding that it didn't match any amplifier you already had, etc, etc – the song was either abandoned completely or played on an electric with the volume backed off.

These days, things are very different indeed. We've already seen that electro-acoustics are more readily available now, but there are other factors that are also on the would-be gigging acoustic player's side:

- Smallish PA systems are far more affordable and a lot of them sound really professional;

- Many live venues have house PA systems that not only work properly but also come with a resident sound engineer who actually knows what he's doing;

- Many amplifier manufacturers have dedicated acoustic amps in their catalogues which, while not as good as PAs, at least don't sound unforgiving and terrible.

Even as recently as ten years ago, none of the above would have been true, so you can count your blessings that you've chosen to perform in a musical environment that has evolved significantly in favour of the acoustic player.

"It all starts with an awareness, and I think that playing onstage with another guitarist is not so different to being the only guitarist onstage and playing with a keyboard player. You have to leave space. You have to have big ears to respond harmonically and rhythmically on the spot and then get out of the way. All you're there to do is to help that soloist perpetuate whatever he's feeling at the time. I think it takes patience and, like I said, big ears and, as I wrote on [my] album, lack of ego. Your motives have to be pure for the music to really come off." *Larry Carlton on playing with other musicians*

Unplugged?
Obviously, the aim of any musician is to be able to give performances that are as consistent as possible, night after night. That, of course, will depend largely on the musician's own state of mind, which is a fragile enough thing in itself. Add to that the vagaries involved in playing venues with grossly differing acoustics, stage sizes, etc, and you can see why some form of consistency is a much-sought-after thing.

One of the ways in which you can adopt some sort of common denominator that you can rely upon gig after gig is to make sure that you're as self-reliant as possible when it comes to sound. Simply turning up at a venue with a guitar and a head full of repertoire is an incredible leap of faith, even in these more enlightened times, so many players are now attempting to rationalise their live sound, literally trying to keep control over it until the last minute before it's sent out into the area in which the artist has no control: the venue's acoustics.

I thought it would be a good idea to have a close look at one artist's acoustic armoury in order to illustrate exactly what lengths it's possible to go to in the name of consistency of sound. Eric Roche is a guitarist who is challenging the boundaries of what's possible with an acoustic guitar, as anyone who has seen him perform will attest.

Eric Roche's Set-Up

A Lowden 010-model guitar with an RMC (Richard McCarthy) Polydrive I combination piezo and MIDI pick-up. The MIDI side of the pick-up is hexaphonic, which means that there is a separate MIDI signal sent from each guitar string.

Also on board the Lowden is a Mimesis Blend system (now called Rare Earth and produced by Fishman) comprising two units: one is an AKG mic inside the guitar itself while the other is a magnetic pick-up across the soundhole.

On The Floor

The MIDI from the RMC pick-up is fed into a Roland GR30 guitar synthesiser and used for very occasional double-bass or sub-bass sounds and faded in using a Boss stereo-volume pedal. Regarding the use of his guitar synth, Eric says, "I don't want to give the impression that the synth is anything but a very small part of my sound. Most of my pieces don't have any synth while the three or four that do only use it for a bit of texture."

Outboard Gear

Korg Toneworks DTR2 Tuner
Roland GP8 (used for chorus only)
Yamaha REV500 (reverb)

Mixer

Eric has never really liked the sound of piezo pick-ups, and so the overall balance from the guitar is around 75 per cent in favour of the Mimesis Blend system. The RMC piezo is used with the bass and boosted to enhance the guitar's bottom end. The outputs from

Eric's guitar are fed into a Mackie 1202 mixer, and so the house PA is fed only left and right stereo signals. This means that Eric is able to keep control of his sound for as long as possible down the signal path until it reaches the venue's PA system.

I'll leave the final word to Eric: "Although it is not 'unplugged', I am still a purist at heart and seek the most authentic acoustic tone I can with this set-up."

Obviously, this is a fairly extreme example of how a top-flight professional player maintains his live sound, but it will give you some idea of what lengths it's possible to go to in order to achieve consistently favourable results. It's a good thing to remember that there's more to performing than simply learning the songs.

Other Live Set-Ups

"I use an AKG C46D condenser microphone with the narrowest capsule they make and I have an acoustic pick-up which they make in a little garage in Nashville that I use to fill it up a little. I hate all those bridge pick-ups; I've not heard one that works. I really don't like the way they sound. They don't sound real to me.

"Onstage, the guitar is fed into a very good microphone pre-amp and from there it goes to the board. The whole band wear ear monitors and so we have a whole lot less stage volume and a lot less feeding back." *Ottmar Liebert*

"I bought a Sennheiser microphone and put it inside the guitar, so I've got a Fishman pick-up and the Sennheiser goes through a pre-amp. I'm using a Lexicon reverb and a Yamaha FX500 just for some chorus on the pick-up." *Antonio Forcione*

"My acoustic is a Martin D18. I think it's about 1970, a nice oldish one. I've got a pick-up – it's a Mimesis. Bill Puplett helped design this one. I think Fishman make it now and call it a Rare Earth. It's got a little microphone built onto the magnetic pick-up with a blend knob on the inside." *Robbie McIntosh*

"I play a variety of guitars, but my main guitars

are Matons, which are made in Australia, and I've played them nearly all my life. Every plane you get onto these days is always really crowded, and so when I travel I take a little AER amplifier with me. I use a little Alesis MIDIverb – that's about it." *Tommy Emmanuel*

"I feed the signal into a pre-amp, which in turn gets fed into the PA. We're experimenting with a little external miking, too, but we really try and keep things simple." *Laurence Juber, Paul McCartney's Wings*

"They made a run of only 90 of these particular guitars [the Gibson J 200 Celebrity model] in 1984/5 and we've now obtained three. Dave just really likes them – they sound great and they're really lovely to play. I've had them modified – they've got EMG acoustic pick-ups in, but they've also got small Crown microphones in them, too, so there are basically two outputs from each guitar, two separate radio transmitters on them with two different signals." *Phil Taylor, Pink Floyd's head of backline, on David Gilmour's acoustic set-up from the 1994 Pink Floyd world tour*

"I'm using a Yamaha APX guitar with the APX pick-up system. I'm also using an AKG microphone on a gooseneck which I've built in, then onto a pre-amp and through a Yamaha FX500, mainly for reverb." *Neil Stacey*

FAMOUS LAST WORDS

"At any given time, you can see me walking up and down the streets of New York with headphones on bawling helplessly, listening to *The King And I* or something, so when it comes to playing the guitar it helps, because I'm a very emotional player." *Steve Vai*

Just before we say our farewells, pick up our party bags and head for the door, I thought it was time for one last curtain-call for some of the celebrity players you've hopefully learned from during the reading of this book. This particular collection of quotes all circle around the theme of playing in general, and I hope they'll offer you further insight and inspiration.

"I was just lucky to be in the right place at the right time and very fortunate to have survived." *Eric Clapton*

"There's no magic. I'm not talented. It's just hard work and persistence." *King Rollo*

"Just go ahead and have fun with it. Be prepared to make mistakes, because that's the way you learn. That's how you find new riffs. Just jam with your friends, make mistakes, step all over your own dick – it doesn't matter. Just have fun, go out and play, have a few beers. It doesn't matter." *Steve Lukather*

"Let's face it, guitarists' solo albums can be among the most boring ever created." *Nick Kane*

"I'm a musician, not the president of the United States or something." *Nuno Bettencourt*

"I don't really [play acoustic guitar]. I have an semi-acoustic guitar that I play on around the house, but I never play it onstage. I played acoustic on a couple of songs on [my] record. I just kind of stuck with the electric thing, although I'm a big fan of the acoustic-guitar players. I was listening to Robert Johnson and the next minute I was listening to Freddy King – and I think Freddy won!" *Robert Cray*

"I'm still being influenced. I'm still drawing back from those times when I was a kid and immersed in the guitar in a different way to how I am now. I love the guitar and I've learned to love it more, but my life is mixed up with a load of other crazy things." *Steve Howe*

"I was with Tchad Blake at Real World doing some music with Peter Gabriel and we wound up at this stone quarry. We basically went and recorded the piece ['Unborn Embrace' from Vernon's *Mistaken Identity* album] with a Pig Nose amp and an E-Bow and we worked 50 feet underground and I improvised little short pieces and then Tchad gave me the tape and said, 'Hey, man, do whatever you want to do.' So I played it in the studio mixing room and [producer] Teo Macero heard it and said, 'You know, I think I have something I did in the same key,' and he turns around and goes into his bag and pulls out a record that he did in 1950 and puts the record on. We did not reharmonise anything; we didn't sample anything; we simply played the record and the DAT at the same time. It was uncanny. It was really freaky, because it sounded OK for the first eight bars, and then 16 bars go by and it's still happening, and 32 bars go by and we were still playing it, and it was like, 'Oh my God!' It was really like a soloist playing with an orchestra." *Vernon Reid*

"We now have this consciousness about sound – everyone is into it and it's very important to make a state-of-the-art record, because it is a very beautiful, sensual, ravishing instrument. You don't want the music to be 'new age'; you want it to have content, but at the same time you must use this sparkling quality of the acoustic." *Andy Summers*

"I find that the best ideas come from when you're not actually touching the guitar. Otherwise your fingers fall into the same positions and you get stuck in ruts." *Brian May*

"I like an ugly guitar!" *Dweezil Zappa*

"Sometimes just change the lyric or change the tuning or the instrument that you try the song on. Pick up something else and do it a different way. Very often, it will dictate something different to you. I often find that what you've written can yield something else." *Mark Knopfler*

"I have always been attracted to the Gypsy style of guitar playing: very physical, very beautiful, and they use a system of scales which is very different from folk or jazz. They've got that Arabic feel, working in quarter-tones by pulling the strings. I've jammed with those guys nearly all night long sometimes and really enjoyed it." *Antonio Forcione*

"My whole attitude is one of perpetual curiosity and studenthood. As much as I love all the music I'm doing with these musicians, equally I love the process of meeting them halfway and seeing how I can approach the thing respectfully and build something beautiful. I'm also finding some interesting things out about master musicians. For one, none of them have any ego; the real masters are totally relaxed, with no ego or insecurity. And it doesn't matter if they're from Hawaii or India, they've all got this hilarious nine-year-old boy sense of humour. At one point, I had Debashisha and his brother playing tablas in Hawaii with Ledward Kaapana and these two guys hit it off great. They were telling fart jokes within the first five minutes!" *Bob Brozman*

"I never could get actual Buddy Guy, real Buddy Guy in the studio. In other words, I've been in studios and it's almost like listening to someone else instead of being myself. During the Chess days, there was Willie Dixon and God knows whoever else teaching me how to play in the studio and so on. Of course, I have myself to blame, too, because I should have said, 'Y'all let me be myself,' but I just don't know how to say no to music! I've been a nut for blues all my life and I just figured... Matter of fact, Dixon used to tell me, and BB King: anything is better than nothing at all, man. Thank God now I'm around and in pretty good health to see myself try and play something pretty well enough for someone to say, 'You sound pretty good.'" *Buddy Guy*

"The thing that attracted me to music in the first place was the emotional side. I was always drawn to music on an emotional basis. The feeling of the music drew me in. It was kind of greed on my part, because I wanted to do some of that for myself. I'd always liked the idea of creating a mood and trying to project that to an audience." *Jim Mullen*

"I make music and it just happens to be on the guitar because that happens to be the instrument that I play." *Joe Satriani*

"This is my life. I mean, it isn't just for money

that I play this; it's what I love, worked really hard at and nurtured. And it hasn't been easy." *John Hammond*

"It was 1959 and I was waiting backstage to go on and the band before me was a five-piece who eventually became The Stoneman Family and they did a version of 'Hey Joe'. It was bluegrass-sounding, some of the lyrics were different, but the pattern was there. I thought the chord pattern was mesmerising, and after I left the air force I heard a guy called Vince Martin playing it and I asked him if he'd written it. He said he'd heard it from some woman in Appalachia a few years before. So I just started developing the song just based on the first line of the lyrics, 'Hey Joe, I heard you shot your woman down', and building it up, taking the bare guts and updating it. I added some lyrics and recorded it with a drummer and the whole thing came together. I never copyrighted it because I was told that it wasn't worth anything. However, I should have gone against the advice I received and done it, because I'd be a little bit more well off today than I am." *Tim Rose, whose version of 'Hey Joe' pre-dated that of Jimi Hendrix by a few years*

"You can't be totally original. You borrow stuff and make it your own, but it's a very elemental type of music. What you try and do is create a feel. But as far as originality is concerned, it's all very intertwined.

"I've tried to come up with some guitar playing which is as devoid of cliché as it can possibly be. I'm really not interested in getting onstage and playing Albert King licks. There are a lot of guys out there who do that, a lot of real purists, and I get kinda bored with it because they seem to me more like mimics than musicians. You might as well be listening to someone impersonate Humphrey Bogart or something!" *Walter Trout*

"I had this deaf grandmother. When my dad bought a television, there was no more radio in our house, no more of my dad playing the piano. When he came home from work, he was going to get his money's worth. So I used to walk four miles up to my grandmother's to listen to The Goons. She hadn't got a clue what I was listening to, so I'd listen to The Goons and then start flicking the dials and finding all these long-wave stations from Europe. A lot of them were especially for the American services and so you'd get Miles Davis, John Coltrane and Hank Williams, and I just fell in love with it, especially if it had a guitar in it. I've remained the same ever since – I don't just listen to one style of music; I listen to all kinds of stuff." *Michael Chapman*

"The guitar hero is sort of dead, in a way. I'm sort of on the end of all that. I'm playing with Sting and we're part of that generation of big-time touring acts that go around the world, but it's changing so rapidly." *Dominic Miller*

ANY QUESTIONS?

If you have any questions or queries relating directly to the content of this book, you can contact David Mead via his website at www.davidmead.net.

While you're there, you'll be able to find out about David's latest publications and keep yourself up to date with his guitar clinics and concert appearances.

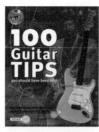

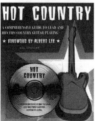